MY TEACHING ROUTINE

To Grace + femi + Alex
Thank for your support.
I hope you enjoy the read
From Mark

Sara Miller McCune founded SAGE Publishing in 1965 to support the dissemination of usable knowledge and educate a global community. SAGE publishes more than 1000 journals and over 800 new books each year, spanning a wide range of subject areas. Our growing selection of library products includes archives, data, case studies and video. SAGE remains majority owned by our founder and after her lifetime will become owned by a charitable trust that secures the company's continued independence.

Los Angeles | London | New Delhi | Singapore | Washington DC | Melbourne

MY TEACHING ROUTINE

Mark Martin

CORWIN

SAGE Publications Ltd
1 Oliver's Yard
55 City Road
London EC1Y 1SP

Corwin
A SAGE company
2455 Teller Road
Thousand Oaks, California 91320
(800)233-9936
www.corwin.com

SAGE Publications India Pvt Ltd
B 1/I 1 Mohan Cooperative Industrial Area
Mathura Road
New Delhi 110 044

SAGE Publications Asia-Pacific Pte Ltd
3 Church Street
#10-04 Samsung Hub
Singapore 049483

Editor: Delayna Spencer
Production editor: Victoria Nicholas
Copyeditor: Jane Fricker
Proofreader: Thea Watson
Marketing manager: Dilhara Attygalle
Cover design: Wendy Scott
Typeset by: C&M Digitals (P) Ltd, Chennai, India
Printed in the UK

Library of Congress Control Number: 2022942316

British Library Cataloguing in Publication data

A catalogue record for this book is available from the British Library

ISBN 978-1-5297-6239-6
ISBN 978-1-5297-6240-2 (pbk)

At SAGE we take sustainability seriously. Most of our products are printed in the UK using responsibly sourced papers and boards. When we print overseas we ensure sustainable papers are used as measured by the PREPS grading system. We undertake an annual audit to monitor our sustainability.

CONTENTS

ABOUT THE AUTHOR

In 2014, Mark Martin MBE aka @urban_teacher, an Assistant Professor in Computer Science and Education Practice, posted a picture of his 'Teaching Routine' on Twitter after teaching for ten years in some of the most challenging schools in the UK. Being observed hundreds of times, his classroom routine always seemed to help him achieve a good or outstanding lesson mark. Even when Ofsted entered his room, they could never find fault with the rapport he has with his learners or his high expectations. Mark decided to create a diagram on PowerPoint to show other professionals what methods he used in his lessons to inspire and motivate his learners. He randomly tweeted the PowerPoint slide out to his Twitter followers and the response was well received by many teachers online.

The 'Teaching Routine' diagram developed when Gaz Needle and Rebeca Zuñiga drew their own interpretations of the teaching model. As a result, the 'Teaching Routine' went viral, and many teachers across the world started asking for resources and guidance on how to use these strategies in their lessons. This was the birth of the 'Teaching Routine', and with the help of educators around the world, we were able to put this book together so teachers everywhere, from rural areas to inner city schools, are able to access this great resource to enhance their teaching and learning in the classroom.

The 'Teaching Routine' takes the teachers and learners through the different stages of a lesson. The steps guide the teacher with setting up activities or scenarios in order for learners to maximise their learning. The learning outcome of the 'Teaching Routine' is to help teachers create excellent learning environments and build genuine connections with learners.

In 2019, Mark was awarded an MBE for services to education, technology, and diversity in UK technology. In May 2022, he was recognised as one of the top 50 most influential people in UK IT by *Computer Weekly*.

ACKNOWLEDGEMENTS

I just want to say a huge thank you to all the global educators and my colleagues who have inspired me to put this book together. Also, I would like to salute my friends and family who have constantly encouraged the work I have been doing in the education sector. Rest in peace to my Aunt Hyacinth Thomas and Uncle Adolphus Thomas, who provided a steady foundation for me to pursue my journey into education. Also a special mention to Dave Martin, my former secondary school teacher, who has guided me throughout the book and shared his thirty years' experience. Lastly, thanks to Ashley Hall, Cardella Bryce, Katherine McLoughin, Osi Ejofor and Bukky Yusuf who shared their personal experiences of being a classroom practitioner.

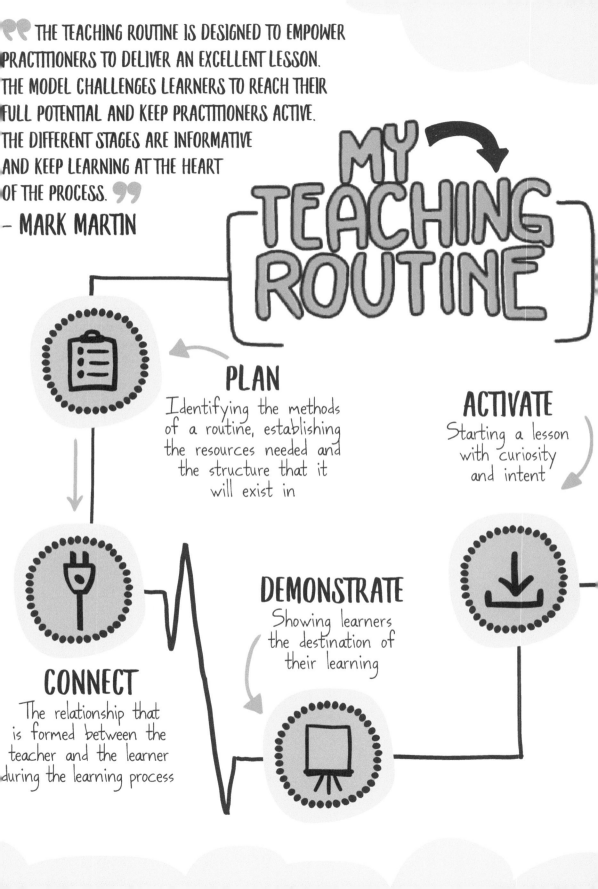

"THE TEACHING ROUTINE IS DESIGNED TO EMPOWER PRACTITIONERS TO DELIVER AN EXCELLENT LESSON. THE MODEL CHALLENGES LEARNERS TO REACH THEIR FULL POTENTIAL AND KEEP PRACTITIONERS ACTIVE. THE DIFFERENT STAGES ARE INFORMATIVE AND KEEP LEARNING AT THE HEART OF THE PROCESS."
– MARK MARTIN

MY TEACHING ROUTINE

PLAN
Identifying the methods of a routine, establishing the resources needed and the structure that it will exist in

ACTIVATE
Starting a lesson with curiosity and intent

DEMONSTRATE
Showing learners the destination of their learning

CONNECT
The relationship that is formed between the teacher and the learner during the learning process

FACILITATE
Guiding learning
from the position
of instructor

COLLABORATE
Getting learners
to work together
seamlessly

REFLECT
Being able
to review your
teaching routine
effectively

CONSOLIDATE
Understanding
progress and

the retaining
of information

INTRODUCTION

My experience as a classroom teacher over a number of years has been used as a starting point to formulate ideas for a teaching framework. I learned to give attention to how I thought and what I said, and not simply what I did in a practical sense. In other words, I engaged in what I call reflective-metacognition, and such reflections will be added to each chapter that covers a part of my teaching routine. However, before I share my teaching routine, let's consider how I will use a range of words throughout the book and I shall begin with the pronoun 'my'.

Who is the 'my' in my teaching routine?

- I am drawing on my personal experiences in this book to help you to think further on your 'my' in your practice. It's about owning your routine and practice, which brings progression.
- An example of 'my' is what happens when a coach gets their athlete to reflect on their own performance. It's about being reflective of every routine you put into place in your teaching.
- The last bullet is combining bullet point one and two, which generates your own 'my' and always reflect.

WHO IS THIS BOOK FOR?

My Teaching Routine aims to take you on a journey. It is not a linear book or one with a fixed narrative sequence which requires you to start at the beginning and work your way through to the end. You can jump in and start from any section you choose and read the different chapters in any order you like.

Newly qualified teacher

For those that are new to the platform of teaching, my teaching model will help to show you the mistakes I have made and areas where my teaching has improved over my experience of practice. You know the idea or concept about talking with, rather than to, your younger self? Well some sections of this book are exactly that: it's like I'm talking with my younger self about all the advice that was not given to me when I first started teaching.

Supply teacher

Supply teachers are continuously having to change their teaching routine to match the cover classes', schools' or agency's needs. The teaching routine will enable you to use different parts of the book to support your practice as you transition through different scenarios within a school environment. Supply teachers don't just cover the base but they ensure learners receive a high quality education.

Experienced teacher

The book speaks to the experienced teacher who needs a new perspective on their practice. Even the best teachers in the field need continuous training and development to enhance their craft as we experience more blended teaching and learning encounters due to Covid-19, more multimodal platforms, and more ways of communicating in and around the classroom with the relentless advances in technology.

Having said that, I believe, like Dr Elizabeth Gemmil on Amol Rajan's 'Rethink Education: Technology and Education' programme (BBC Sounds, 2021), that technology should be used to enhance understanding not just replace conventional ways of understanding things, or put simply, technology should not be a means of using a computer in the place of a teacher. I hope the book challenges you to revisit some of your 'bias blind spots' and reflect on those lessons or periods in your teaching that did not go well. This book also deals with the ways in which I have managed to get the learners to engage and connect with studying.

School leaders

The book supports school leaders in motivating their staff to do better and be better in the classroom. Let me make a brief distinction here between a leader and a manager. A leader empowers and guides their staff whereas a manager has people who work for them. An effective leader is able to provide a clear vision that is easy to translate to others around them. This is done through getting teachers to see a broader perspective of their practice, i.e. the 50,000 feet view is better than a limited tunnel vision perspective. I believe that leaders need to lead from the front with empathy and compassion, and promote togetherness throughout the institution consistently. Good leadership will seek to foster negotiated dialogue spaces, where leaders work with staff to listen to their concerns about classroom teaching experiences. The book is not about providing quick fix answers but giving leaders more opportunities to form learning dialogues with their colleagues. In a nutshell, the book is for those with an open mindset for change and doing things differently.

WHY 'LEARNERS'?

I am particular about lexical choice. Throughout the book I chose the word 'learners' instead of 'students'. Why? Because the label or address term 'learners' provides a broader, more holistic context when I am talking about the young people we teach and interact with in educational settings.

HOW DOES THIS BOOK HELP?

INTRODUCTION

IMPACT   MENTAL HEALTH   POST-PANDEMIC
                & WELLBEING

The book aims to take you out of your comfort zone, to constantly review your teaching style, and as a teacher, to challenge you to ask a series of questions such as:

- What **impact** does my current style of teaching have on the learning of those in the educational spaces I am responsible for?
- What is the correlation between my teaching style and my **wellbeing and mental health**?
- How will my teaching practice evolve **post-pandemic**?

Recent books on teaching promote putting learners first; yet teachers need to be put first because a burnt out teacher is no good to anyone. Teachers need to detect when things are going well, and when things need to change through reflection and feedback on their practice. There should be more spaces and opportunities for teachers to share their insights and good practice with others within the profession. The book promotes spaces for you to learn, unlearn and relearn approaches to teaching and learning; it is a straightforward statement to make but challenging to put into practice. My ideas in the book are not limited to a focus on the classroom. No. I draw on examples from everyday life; and just like a seventeenth-century metaphysical poet using a conceit, I make far-fetched yet relevant comparisons, drawing from 'everyday life', a range of experiences and a range of disciplines. Why? Simply, because education should be a rich universal experience.

The text is a continual piece or holistic text that you can use to challenge and probe the 'why' in your teaching practice. I hope the book encourages you to lead learners into a wider world of knowledge and not to be disheartened if you get things wrong, or rather, if things do not turn out as you expect after one attempt. I embrace the view that for most of my teaching career I have been learning from mistakes and mishaps, those beyond my control, and seeing them as material for feedback to improve my practice, and not as being in a rut of fatigued failure.

SETTING THE TONE

It is my belief that the classroom reflects the universe, and there are no real boundaries to knowledge, creativity and innovation. Learning should not exist for assessment. Learning outcomes are much more than exams and grades and data for progress grades. No. Learning outcomes are about the connections, events, memories, conversations and relationships. Learning is about being present, generating new ideas, and the list goes on. And learning is not just about the learners benefiting; teachers should teach in psychological spaces where they benefit as well. Every child matters; every teacher matters. Having a teaching routine provides clarity on the things we need to do to raise the aspiration and attainment in the classroom and for ourselves.

There are several things to consider when using the teaching routine:

Physical learning space

The way tables and chairs are positioned in a classroom can shape your teaching routine. Also the way learners enter the physical space can define how calmly the lesson begins. I am aware of the limitation of space in some schools but even with the physical limitations classroom layout should have a focus on learning rather than putting in a teaching routine to enforce control and containment.

The pandemic added another layer of complexity to the teaching routine model because it removed the physical space to an online environment. As a result, the focus then went towards learners' morale, wellbeing and mental health.

Learners' needs – Maslow

Maslow's hierarchy of learning needs is a popular theory published by Abraham Maslow, an American psychologist in 1940s (Maslow, 1943). The theory is a simple framework which reminds us that all learners are less likely to achieve if their basic needs are not being met. The teaching routine acknowledges that the learners' wellbeing (i.e. sleep, hydration and nutrition) and learning behaviour will have an effect on the lesson. Before adequate learning can take place learners' personal needs must be supported. Due to the Covid-19 pandemic and the media's focus on well-being there is now much greater consideration given to each learner's mental health and state of mind.

The teacher's approach to learning

The teaching routine highlights a wide range of pedagogies, such as spaced practice, interleaving, dual coding, retrieval practice and cognitive load, to enhance the standard of teaching and learning.

School and government demands

Schools and teaching routines do not work in silos. There are many demands on a school from following Ofsted guidelines, to school league tables, having low exclusions and reputation.

Not forgetting the ramping up of achievement and attainment for all learners in schools, there is also the issue of avoiding off-rolling of disruptive learners.

KEYWORDS

1. Connect: The relationship that is formed between the teacher and the learner during the learning process
2. Demonstrate: Showing learners the destination of their learning
3. Activate: Starting a lesson with curiosity and intent
4. Facilitate: Guiding learning from the position of instructor
5. Collaborate: Getting learners to work together seamlessly
6. Consolidate: Understanding progress and retaining information
7. Reflect: Being able to review your teaching routine effectively

USE A NOTEBOOK TO TRACK YOUR ROUTINE

In order to get the most out of this book I recommend that you make notes on your progress, like using a journal, as you try, experiment, and test some of the ideas presented in the book.

SHARING IS CARING

If you want to share the different stages of your teaching routine you can use the hashtag #myteachingroutine on social media and don't forget to tag me @urban_teacher for a like and repost.

CHAPTER 1
CONNECT

 Learners buy into the teacher before they buy into the learning. - Mark Martin

OVERVIEW

THIS CHAPTER EXPLORES THE FOLLOWING IDEAS:

* THE FIRST ENGAGEMENT THAT YOU HAVE WITH YOUR LEARNERS SETS THE TONE FOR THE LESSON AND CLASS ENVIRONMENT
* SETTING THE BOUNDARIES AT THE BEGINNING OF THE LESSON HELPS LEARNERS TO HAVE STRUCTURE AND A CLEAR PATH TO FOLLOW
* HAVING CLEAR EXPECTATIONS AT THE START OF EVERY LESSON CREATES CONSISTENCY AND FAMILIARITY FOR LEARNERS
* ISSUING LOW STAKES ACTIVITIES AT THE START OF THE LESSONS HELPS LEARNERS TO BUILD CONFIDENCE AND LONG-TERM MEMORY

Connecting with your learners is the first point of building a rapport between the learner and you, and the learners engaging with the subject beyond your classroom. This triangular relationship of learner, teacher and subject makes it easier to build the foundation of a learning community. The learner–teacher–connection with the subject is the start of a productive relationship, and learners connecting with their peers reinforces a learning community. This aspect of connecting is challenged with online teaching and learning, and we will consider that dynamic later in the book.

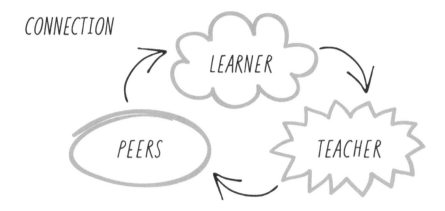

The general point here is that it is the teacher who has a critical role in role modelling positive connections and teaching their learners to do the same. Pigford states teachers must first recognise the importance of positive teacher–learner relationships, then develop definitive strategies to make that relationship happen (Pigford, 2001).

In order to form an effective relationship with our learners, we have to challenge our own perceptions, biases, agenda and expectations that we may have towards our learners. Let's pause here.

- What do we really think about the demographics associated with the learners that we teach or are responsible for? *What do we really think?* Are we fair and respectful towards them and their families? Fair in front of them, and fair behind their back?
- What are our biases, our real biases towards our learners?

According to Fiedler, biases in judgements and decision making that are commonly explained in terms of the individuals prior experiences can already have been formed in unbiased environmental learning (Fiedler et al., 2002). We have to be mindful that our own perceptions of our learners do not hinder the classroom relationship. Developing genuine connection with learners may be a continual process rather than something we do once and for all in a moment in time. To make a connection between a learner and a class, you need to ensure the connection is genuine and meaningful for all parties involved; it will not work if it is one sided.

CONNECTION ANALOGY

To provide an illustration on the topic I'll use the following analogy:

> Connection is like a plug socket, the mains is the safe environment which consists of bound-aries, high expectations and empathy. The learner is the appliance and the teacher is the hand that connects everything together with rapport, subject knowledge and presence. Once the connection is established it illuminates the classroom and culture.

EMPATHY IN CONNECTION

Irrespective of the learner's situation, teachers need to lead with empathy and understanding in order to build rapport with learners. It could be a simple acknowledgement, or creating a small conversation. This adds to the foundation for the classroom connection, even if it's another teacher that teaches that learner. We have explored connection in the broader sense, let's now delve into connection within the classroom context. It could be argued that the connection at the start of the lesson is one of the most important elements of teaching and learning. The start of the lesson can be very unpredictable because it is based on a range of different factors known and unbeknown to the teacher. These include low energy levels, poor working memory and concentration, learner attitudes to studying in a school environment, emotional agitations, the state of learner relation-ships within the group and other groups in the school, or simply the time of day the lesson starts. Learners may even be engrossed in their own conversations about their own business. For some learners finishing a conversation is more important than the learning that should be taking place. And let's not forget what might happen en route to a lesson via a crowded corridor. Normally, the lesson planning, classroom management and seating plans will help to resolve some of these issues. Also, just a moment of silence can help the learner work with you in the connect-ing process and help them to focus should disruptions take place. Do not underestimate the role of silence before commencing or during an activity. Schultz states, assuming the primacy of talk over silence, we should consider silence a form of participation, and learn how it works in our classroom. Attention to silence alongside talk will lead to more equitable classrooms that hold the possibility of honouring the contributions of all learners (Schultz, 2012).

However we are aware that some learners may want to test or even challenge the strength of connection by not following known and familiar instructions. The challenge from the learner might even be aimed at disrupting the class and breaking down levels of established order, and even bringing disruptive allies along with them. When this happens the teacher may need to speak to the rest of the class to set clear boundaries and repeat expectations; and then, using the appropriate tone, speak to the learner who has chosen to leave the established path for connecting and use class management techniques to bring the disruptor back into an established boundary. This means the teacher needs to have pre-existing clear boundaries and expectations to keep the whole class focused. It's important the teacher stays calm and chooses the right words; the appropriate pace and tone should be effective to keep the class connected and invite those with weak connections to re-connect. However, staying calm and doing the right thing when things go wrong at the start of a lesson is, in my view, one of the biggest challenges in teaching a lesson. Why? Because you might lose some of the learners for the entire lesson.

A popular public figure, Sims Wyeth, wrote an article on the best way to hold people's attention. He states:

> Listeners interpret everything a speaker does: they read your face, your inner rhythm, your posture, voice, and stance. In fact, the human mind ascribes moral intention to physical cues having the slightest hint of emotional expression. The problem is the mind does this in a matter of seconds, and you have to speak longer than that. Plus you may be nervous, not at your scintillating best, so your technical skill at capturing and holding attention could be the difference between success and failure. Every business presentation will have plenty of moments when the audience will have to work hard and pay attention to grasp the material. I am suggesting that your results, and your reputation, will improve when your audience finds you and your content fascinating. (Wyeth, 2014)

Sims' reflection is very powerful in reading the room and knowing his audience. When we are at the front of the classroom do we go into auto pilot mode and just teach, or do we feel the vibe of the room?

Let's explore how a comedian and doctor approach the same situation.

COMEDIAN TRAVIS JAY AND DOCTOR KATRINA SHEIKH – PERSONAL EXPERIENCES

Comedian Travis Jay has the notion of establishing trust at the start of his comedy routine. He points to the significance of first impressions – as we know you get one chance to make a first impression – and Travis refers to the image of a pilot and passengers on a plane. When asked how he engages a room Travis responds, 'I think about the confidence that a pilot has to instil when he or she makes an announcement at the beginning of a flight … that's how people are with their imagination … if they feel that they can trust you, then they'll go with you wherever you're taking them.' Failure to do so is likely to instil panic. In his role as a comedian Travis will re-try if his audience is actively disengaged. 'The first 15 secs is important because you will need to make a quick decision to reset or continue with your performance. I won't go into a long story if they are not coming with me, so I need to get their attention by asking them something trivial i.e. name, hobbies, etc.'

He adds, 'Before I can get to my message, I have to establish a human connection … Once I have found some common ground then I start my comedy act.'

Acute medical doctor Katrina Sheikh, who promotes a compassionate and caring style of leadership, practises an unconventional approach to connecting with patients who are not willing to listen and who are reluctant to comply with support whilst under care or who refuse to take advice from medical staff. In November 2021 Katrina was leading the ward round and recalls meeting a patient for the first time. The patient had been homeless for more than 15 years, drug dependent for a number of years, suicidal, and happened to be the most 'cachexic person' she'd ever seen. This patient refused medical support; he was aggressive and violent to staff nurses, etc. After reading his medical notes and listening to warnings from her colleagues about the patient, Katrina still wanted to connect with the patient. She took a novel approach which included pulling up a chair (but would kneel if there were no chairs available), and getting eye level with this patient (instead of looking down at him from above whilst the patient lay on the bed, which is the conventional way and known to be 'quite intimidating' for patients). Katrina introduced herself without using her full title or surname; in linguistics we would label this as accommodation theory, where the speaker converges to aid communication rather than diverging and creating a barrier to maintain social distance. She noticed his accent and made a connection because they both had a link with that part of the country. They spoke about the region for the first five minutes or so and she then asked him how he was, how he had got here, what his concerns were. Katrina adds, 'I automatically had that trust.' She made him a better cup of tea, which was unlike the weak, milky brew she found when she got down to eye level with this patient. For Katrina being honest, or as entertainer J.Lo would say, 'Keeping it real', and using her emotional intelligence to imagine how scary it was for the patient made a difference. 'I think it's really important to mirror who you're talking to, get down on their level, ask them, engage in actively listening, give them time to talk … and don't follow it by the book sometimes which doctors have always been told to do.' The outcome in this anecdote was that the patient agreed to have the scans and, going forward, trust the medical staff.

These examples, from Travis Jay and from Doctor Katrina Sheikh, about connecting to reluctant listeners or those who are disengaged, highlight the importance of understanding your audience on a 'human level' and the steps you take to gain a sense of trust. Reducing the distance between parties makes communication easier and the possibility of connecting greater. Reading the room or space makes it easier to adjust and work towards making the connection work. For us, the onus is on the teacher to initiate the connection and be willing to re-try so that learners are involved. Teachers have influence and a growing skill set to make a difference, and let's not forget that being honest and keeping it real gives you a sense of confidence that overrides challenges to the disconnection.

PRACTICAL WAYS TO CONNECT

Greeting learners by their name, making eye contact, or stating the expectations of what you want to see by the end of the lesson are effective connecting techniques. Whether your class size is large or small you could consider the need to select a few learners that need encouragement or clear instructions. Don't underestimate the power of positive words and expressions when getting learners to follow your instructions. I will normally look for the smallest thing to praise so the learner is aware I'm acknowledging them; but don't over-praise or use prosaic features deemed to be patronising. Sometimes I like to probe a little bit further by asking learners about their day so far and what one positive thing they would like to achieve by the end of the lesson. This creates a solid connection and holds them to account on the targets they set for themselves.

Before learners sit down, I ask them to stand behind their chair and wait for the next set of instructions. This lets them know boundaries are in place and they have to follow my lead. Some learners may protest because you may be the only teacher that has this routine or they want to test the boundary. In order for this to work you need to be consistent and demand learners follow the routine you have put in place. By 'reading the room', you can tell by the learners' response whether they are engaging positively or negatively towards your instructions. Also, significant clues (Davis, 1984) are found in the learners' body language, and from such clues teachers can read whether they are engaged or disengaged. The teacher can then use these cues to encourage learners to commence the activity. The aim is to create a calm start to the lesson where the teacher is in control of the space and environment. The teacher sets the tempo, so learners can mirror and follow. The pace of engagement is underpinned by the lesson content and instructions. The rhythm of the lesson starts to become clear and easy to follow for learners and anyone who enters the room. Your pace and tempo if done consistently becomes the melody that learners follow without prompting. It works! Once learners are seated, I normally set three targets in a tick box format that they need to achieve before the lesson ends. This helps them to monitor their progress and manage their learning.

PLANNING

Lesson planning with engagement in mind is critical for setting classroom culture and connecting with learners. The process can be very time consuming and a lonely experience if you are working on your own. There are a few shortcuts in lesson planning, either purchasing a SoW (Scheme of Work) or collaborating with other educators within your teacher learning network. Lesson planning should be like Lego bricks, where you have a range of mini activities which you can build on throughout the learning experience.

Here are the elements you need to build an effective teaching routine:

SoW: The short-term, medium- and long-term plan helps to keep you focused on what needs to be covered throughout the academic year. The content needs to be engaging, relevant and incremental, so learners understand the journey you want to take them on. To get the most of SoWs, plan to break up the content into stages or levels so learners can measure their progress at the start of the topic and how well they are doing as the weeks proceed.

Meaningful work: Plan and design meaningful work for learners so it develops their soft skills and academic skills. The aim is to then be able to transfer these skills across different subjects or explain to others the concepts they have learned in your lessons. I would normally challenge my learners to go home and educate one person in their household about the terminologies they had learned in my lesson. This helps to strengthen their academic and soft skills.

Differentiation: In most, if not all, classes you are likely to have different abilities and ways that learners access the content in your classroom. The concept and practice of differentiation is important for connecting with your learners. Matching the starter activity to the learner's ability helps them to keep focused on the task. Don't underestimate how you can use the starter to set the tone and structure of your lesson. Differentiation is important to connecting with your learners; in a class you will have different abilities.

Resources: There are a variety of ways of generating resources for our lessons, from creating content to purchasing SoWs on the web. The most important element of resources is that they are relevant, engaging and challenging for our learners. The questions I normally ask myself are: Are the resources connected to the real world or future of work? Or do they relate to learners' interests or hobbies for better engagement? Whenever I connect the two it seems learners produce better work and retain information better. It's very difficult to tailor every lesson to learners because it takes a lot of time in a profession where time is limited to do creative things. My advice would be not to reinvent the wheel and see whether other educators are using new creative resources in their lessons. If not then it might be useful to develop some resources which are current and relevant to students.

Practical vs theoretical learning : Theoretical learning is normally the default way to teach a lesson, because it's imparting knowledge and information for learners to digest and store in their long-term memory. Many learners have to acclimatise to this way of teaching, but it's limited in providing learners with a full scope of the skills they are trying to use in their everyday activities and exams. Practical learning provides a hands-on experience which helps the learner to connect to the content they are learning. To plan regular practical lessons can be tricky if the subject is centred around literature and key concepts. I guess it's about creating a balance between theoretical and practical learning to keep learners connected.

WHY DO LEARNERS DISCONNECT?

There are many factors why learners may connect with or conversely disconnect from their learn-ing. These include the learner's ability in the subject, the perception of the subject and education as a whole, their attitude towards learning in school, and the overall school experience. Irrespective of the learner's situation, it's imperative the teachers form genuine connections to foster rich learn-ing environments throughout the school, and these connections are both what I call formal and informal connections which can occur in and out of the classroom. Informal talk or 'real' talk where the learner might set the agenda to lead the conversation gives them a voice and identity to be themselves. This can be established in their tutor group, coaching group or school meetings. Also it can be initiated in the school library or in lunch-time and after-school clubs. A common place for connecting is the corridors or the playground, even when a teacher is on a type of duty. It could be a genuine greeting, a simple acknowledgement, a brief conversation on mutual hobbies or interests. It could be a series of walk-and-talk connections en route to lessons. These informal con-nections can set the foundation for the classroom connection. Formal connections are in specified spaces like assemblies or in formal learning spaces where formal lessons take place and the talk is subject based, educational, and where the power relations are less negotiated for the learner. For both meaningful informal or formal connection to take place there has to be respect, appropri-ate language usage and tone, body language and so on. Setting up the mindset for connecting should be done and cross-supported by all staff – that's teaching and non-teaching staff – in the school community; and that means avoiding confrontational language, or even at times too much regulatory language, inside or outside of the classroom.

Knuppenburg and Fredericks' study suggests that the positive use of language and communica-tion has profound effects on emotional mental health. The language we use can shape learners' self-perception and evaluations of others (Knuppenburg and Fredericks, 2021). Leah Shafer goes one step further and suggests a positive school culture consists of the common language used, exemplifying the beliefs, values, strength in relationships and respect for diversity in the community.

Words such as tolerance, empathy, diversity and respect are not only spoken, but acted out with authenticity (Leah Shafer, 2018). It's crucial school leaders cultivate a learning environment where mutual respect is formed in and of the classroom; and all staff – teaching and non-teaching – buy into this culture.

However, as noted above, learners' disconnect from school or their learning can stem from their ability, perception of education, attitude towards learning or general school experience. As Jennie Hanna argues, students are coming to school with issues that affect the way in which they learn or behave within a classroom. These issues may include neglect, poverty, a lack of social skills, an unstable support system, or even a disillusioned concept of school as a whole. It may be worth stating some learners may even exhibit anti-school issues that are generated from their own parents' or carers' anti-school experience. Issues may even stem from the learner's self-perception or anxiety regardless of their socio-economic background. These issues can result in students who appear disengaged and unmotivated to participate in their own learning (Hanna, 2014).

ANXIETY AND EMOTIONS

Teachers' emotions, mindset and mental health have been only vaguely covered in academic research, compared to the discourse on learners' learning and achievement (Pekrun and Linnenbrink-Garcia, 2014). Hargreaves argues emotions are at the heart of education; they are linked to the teachers' wellbeing, quality of teaching and what they feel about their learners. Good teaching is powered by positive emotions (Hargreaves, 2005). In the last decade, the concerns about the mental health and wellbeing of school teachers have increased in prominence. According to the Nuffield Foundation, one in 20 teachers in England are reporting long lasting mental health problems and their wellbeing has declined over the past three decades (Jerrim et al., 2020); and that's not to mention physical and health challenges like infrequent voiding syndrome where teachers delay urinating for extended periods of time.

The politicising of education for votes by mainstream politicians has whipped up hysteria about falling standards, via league tables, and claims that education needs to be far more rigorous for schools to compete on the global stage (Finn, 2016). Burgess and Thomson's research into the attainment gap between disadvantaged learners and their peers indicates that standards have slightly improved since the introduction of Britain's GCSE reforms in 2015 (Burgess and Thomson, 2019). These have led to further ramping up of the standards on attainment and achievement for schools around the country. Subsequently, Senior Leadership Teams have passed on this hysteria of fear to classroom teachers, and many teachers are now given performance targets that they need to achieve through the academic year. Unfortunately, such targets have been handed down rather than classroom teachers participating in the negotiation of targets for their learners. These targets may include exam results, department results, and whole school contributions. There may be a myriad of reactions and feelings to such targets. With all of these pressures, the scope of the challenge may be exciting, daunting or overwhelming. It may feel like there are a million tick boxes to complete at the start of the lesson, and crucially, before the teacher has made a connection with their learners.

In real terms, a teacher could lose the focus of the value of connecting and just aim to plough through a lesson, tick boxes, and discipline any learner who stands in the way of ticking boxes. Keeping your emotions and expectations in check under such pressures, and let's face it, such pressure at times appears to be relentless, means that such stress will not be transferred to the learners, and will reassure learners that you are in control and you have their best interests at heart. Learners sometimes feed off our emotions and mirror them back to us whether it's positive or negative. Connecting with learners requires teachers to be cool, calm and collected because any unforeseen issue might arise at the start of the lesson, or indeed any stage of a lesson. Understanding the power of emotional intelligence provides you with a range of techniques to manage your emotions (Hagenauer et al., 2015). It's very easy to be derailed from the lesson plan and routine due to settling the class; this can be stressful and discouraging. In 2014, Ofsted published a report stating learners are potentially losing up to an hour of learning each day to low level disruption in the classroom. This adds up to over 38 days of teaching lost per year (Ofsted, 2014). There is a time and space to deal with disruptions at the start of the lesson; it's important to know when to respond and deal with the situation accordingly. Just like a music conductor, their main role is to unify performers, set the tempo, listen critically and shape the sound of the ensemble, and to control the interpretation and pacing of the music. In order for you to keep the pacing of the lesson, your mental health and wellbeing need to be in check by making room for errors and avoiding putting pressure on yourself to get everything right. Have a sense of tolerance for errors. Some of the best lessons I've taught have never gone to plan, but forming the bond meant irrespective of the learners' attitude towards things beyond their control, they were willing to engage. On the other hand, some of the worst lessons I've taught were when I lost focus and I allowed my emotions to dictate my decisions, which led to poor judgement and unrealistic expectations. The point here is never underestimate mental health in your teaching practice; it is influential and a controlling feature of a lot more of your lessons than the actual content (Mayer and Salovey, 1997: 5). Additionally, if you ever feel like things are not going your way then it might be useful to seek help or change your style of engagement.

THE RECIPE TO CONNECTING

The recipe for connecting is the relationship developed between the teacher and learners. At the heart of a genuine relationship is trust, respect and positive reinforcement. This provides a safety net for learners to engage with the lesson activity and connect with the process positively. Clear communication about learning is crucial, and the teacher's part of focusing on the learning is a priority.

However, these learning priorities can easily be derailed by so-called uniform infringements, the learner's micro-movements, or even vocal nonverbal communications. These 'minor' misdemeanours may not necessarily disrupt setting up the 'connecting' for the lesson, but the teacher becoming easily focused on behaviour may inadvertently end up undermining the creation of the/a rich learning environment. Things can quickly deteriorate if teachers respond negatively when learners challenge their authority, when under pressure or when facing a difficult situation. By responding negatively, I mean arguing, confronting or sending the learner out of the room. My rule of thumb is to be professional, manage or navigate your emotions, and try to read the emotions that are being displayed in front of you. This gives you a great clarity on how to respond to the matter and whether action needs to be taken immediately or at a later point. The aim is not to be derailed and lose the connection with the whole class. There's an old saying, 'The fire brigade doesn't put out any fires by pouring more fire onto the situation. They look for the nearest water supply outlet to use to diffuse the fire before it escalates.' Prosodic features such as your tone, your pitch and the rhythm of your speech, your body language, even your gaze are crucial here when it comes to responding to anything that will derail the start of your lesson. There is no weakness in letting learners appear to be breaking the connection because staying in control to better manage the direction of the lesson is more important. The initial instruction given can be the make or break for some learners and how they engage in that part of the lesson. They will either switch off, switch on, or go on auto pilot mode depending on how accessible the learning instruction you have provided is. This is another check-in on how the teacher's use of language is crucial because some learners are coming to school with fringe knowledge topics (i.e. social injustices, geo politics or cryptocurrencies), but the majority of the time they are not starting from ground zero. Teachers need to check previous understanding and knowledge on topics because it's a very easy way to engage and connect learners to the learning. Lucariello and Naff argue when teachers provide instruction on concepts in various subjects, they are teaching students who already have some pre-instructional knowledge about the topic. Learners' knowledge can be erroneous, illogical or misinformed. These erroneous understandings are termed alternative conceptions, misconceptions or intuitive theories. Alternative misconceptions are not unusual. In fact, they are a normal part of the learning process (Lucariello and Naff, 2010). Teachers need to be adaptable and leave space in their instructions for learners to challenge and explore. This takes time to perfect but allows the teacher and student to form a learning dialogue during the connecting stage. I have learned to reduce a lengthy and long winded instruction like over-explaining the lesson objectives whilst learners are in a passive state. In contrast, a clear instruction of what needs to be achieved, backed up with a starter activity to get them instantly engaged, tends to captivate learners. The challenge here is to be consistent with these short snappy activities so it becomes a normalised experience for learners. The fascinating thing about language and instructions is not all learners interpret them the same; and this will be an ongoing challenge in all communication. Also your word choice, emotional state, your perceived body language, breathing, pace, and movement in the learning space can significantly alter the instruction. Some teachers may become anxious that learners haven't understood their instruction and that anxiety can lead to frustration on the teacher's part, but it's imperative that teachers are mindful of their conduct. It is important to be patient with this stage of the lesson.

MY ZEN MODE

The best moments in my career are when I have been in 'Zen Mode'. I'll define this as a state of feeling positive, remaining composed and calm irrespective of the situation. At this optimal state I can engage with learners with both my emotions and my mood in check. The worst scenario is when you are under pressure or in a rush to get through the instructions, which creates frustration if the learners don't respond as you would expect and they tap into your impatience. Explaining instructions in a calm and reassuring manner may help to engage learners better because you have created room for them to get involved. There are lots of clichés being thrown around in education, for example new teachers not smiling before Christmas; really? Is that advice really good? I know the sentiment includes not allowing yourself to seem too familiar to the learners, but surely not smiling or connecting in a humane way works against the idea of establishing good connections and relationships.

 HINTS & TIPS

Here are a few questions to help you think about connecting with your learners:

- **When starting a lesson what's the first thing that comes to mind? Giving out the instruction or checking in on your learners?**
- **Do you connect with your learners before the learning?**
- **What have you found is the most useful way to connect with your learners?**

ACADEMIC CONNECTION

Forming an academic connection with your learners is to continually check learners' understanding and how they are processing the information. You might want to diversify, scaffold or differentiate the instructions as the lesson progresses. Learners' response and feedback is a great cue to inform you whether the instructions have been interpreted effectively and well received. There are many forms of academic connection beyond giving out clear, and timely, instructions at the start of a lesson. Setting a low stakes quiz on prior knowledge, which I will further explore in this chapter, may help to boost confidence and self-esteem as they begin their learning. This kind of recapping from the previous lesson or ideas from earlier lessons is very useful. There isn't a set or specific formula to connect with learners but the approach you decide to take will require time, patience, empathy and consistency. This is easier said than done but with small steps of progress, anything is possible. Small amounts of progress over a long period of time is the main driver to see productivity, engagement and enthusiasm from your learners. I should state that not every school or classroom is identical, nor should they be. Classrooms are very different in terms of context and challenges. Schools are formed of different learning spaces. Your classroom is unique and you have a say in its essence, and how you connect may shift and become better and stronger, but always, the value of connecting should be the priority at the start of every lesson.

HINTS & TIPS

Here are a few tips on how I engage my learners at the start of the lesson. The aim is to get the learners focused on you and the instructions you want them to follow.

1. Smile
2. Make and maintain good eye contact
3. Greet them by name; this may require extra effort to pronounce all of their names correctly
4. State your expectations for the lesson; be commanding and concise
5. State a positive thing they did last lesson and how it can be used to build/aid learning for the present lesson; but this must be brief

LOW STAKES TESTING

A range of activities could be used once you have the attention of the learners and they have set-tled into the lesson. This stage could be labelled the final point of connecting. It might be useful to test their prior knowledge with low stakes questions. This can be done with up to five questions on the topic covered in the previous lesson, and should take five minutes to complete on their own. These questions can be verbal or written. If written, and the answers require additional work, it might prove useful to allow them to correct their answers so they get into the habit of independent marking. Sometimes the questions could be open-ended and the answers could be negotiated, so there are possibilities for what could be labelled 'learning-dialogues'. Probing questions are set by the teacher and there is scope for the learner to offer a response that is indi-vidual. This can establish a teacher and learner bond, which can produce rich learner–teacher conversations. You might get some learners to present their answers to their peers or in front of the whole class to encourage their public speaking skills. Developing confidence in answering questions and expressing their ideas in the class is a very important skill that needs to be devel-oped over time, and is supported by the Oracy Project 2021 (Education Endowment Foundation, 2019). Helping learners to connect to short snappy activities encourages self-regulation because it gets them into a routine of focusing on the subject content, and managing their effort in a range of settings. The high stakes exam culture doesn't help matters, as teachers are guided to 'teach to the test', which adds on additional pressure and anxiety. Using low stakes activities can help to boost learners' self-esteem and help to boost their morale and perspective (Schrum and Hong, 2002) on their academic ability, exams and confidence. The key to low stakes test-ing is to create at least a term's worth of questions and answers so that you can use them on a weekly basis, which creates a routine for the class. Another way to test prior knowledge is to give learners highlighter pens to highlight in their book or on a handout the key concepts they have learned in green, amber for the ones they need to go over again, and red for the ones they have forgotten. You may want to tweak your connect routine so it works for you in your practice. Also, constantly monitor the impact on your learners that your connect activity has made.

 HINTS & TIPS

Here are some practical routines to create lesson structure:

1. **Greet**
2. **Seating plan/register**
3. **Stand behind chairs**
4. **Low stakes activity**
5. **Self-marking**
6. **Start the lesson**

PERSONAL EXPERIENCE

In my first year in teaching I was under the impression that I needed to be a perfectionist in the way I planned and prepared for virtually every lesson. I believed that was the virtue of teaching. I placed a lot of pressure on myself to perform and create outstanding lessons. How wrong were my predictions! As soon as I entered the classroom to deliver the content, I was doubly nervous, then full of anxiety, and this emotional overload compounded my lack of classroom management. And, this cycle was repeated more times than I cared to experience! Within seconds the learners would normally pick up on my emotional aura, and to tell the truth, I was revealing more of my inner unsettled state than I wanted to reveal. It wasn't long before I knew that I was losing the battle to control the class, rapidly. And they knew too.

My impression that learners would follow my class instructions without necessarily forming a connection or having a rapport was wrong. This was a clear blind spot and misconception. I learned that it was the learners who were seeking to form a bond before they followed any of my instructions. After a space of 12 weeks, a full term, I realised and began to relish the value of reflecting on all stages of my general approach and my classroom experience. On reflection I needed to build greater connections with my learners at the start of the lesson. Developing mutual respect and trust, coupled with a positive attitude on my part, would encourage engagement when I gave the learners instructions to follow. In addition, once I realised the power of routines and connections at the start of the lesson, I made it a personal goal to connect with the learners in all of my lessons. This involved getting them to stand behind their chairs, playing a motivational video clip or getting them to present what they had learned from the previous lesson. Connecting became the norm for me and, as in Malcolm Gladwell's words, 'practice makes permanent' (Gladwell, 2008), it became a valued feature of starting my lessons. I'll be honest with you, the process did take several attempts and lots of reflecting on the impact these changes were making on the class. Once I overcame the implementation phase of my routines at the start of the lesson, the results and atmosphere was transformed across all of my teaching groups. I was able to reflect on my practice and use the feedback to improve the delivery. My next challenge was to see if these changes were picked up in formal and informal observations of my lessons, and whether staff were willing to adopt some of my good practice in their own lessons. The feedback from my colleagues was very positive and I was able to share some of my insights with the whole school.

ANOTHER TEACHER'S EXPERIENCE: DAVE MARTIN (ENGLISH STUDIES TUTOR, KS2–KS5)

A challenging experience was when I found myself, quite unexpectedly, in a special needs school on long-term English supply teaching, before securing a permanent job there. I had to make major adjustments and absorb facts and nuances about autistic secondary school learners, and do so quickly.

My Year 10 class was a group of boys; there were seven of them in the class. The ability range was vast: two of the group were working towards the IGCSE qualification in the following academic year yet with their own trials; the majority of the class had reading and writing challenges; and one learner worked with the teaching assistant (this learner amongst other things was learning the English alphabet – and due to his working memory – he would struggle or even forget how to pronounce the letter 'a' or 'cee' independently by the time he was assisted to identify the letter 'kay'). As a new teacher in this SEN school how did I connect with learners with such a wide range of ability in my Year 10 English class? There was no easy or universal answer to that question, and if I had just started out in teaching I would not have considered doing what I ended up doing to connect with these Year 10 learners.

At the outset of this experience, I decided to reflect on my demeanour and communication skills, and learn about the space I found myself in. I worked to remain calm regardless of the things I witnessed; I tried to speak clearly and modify the way I framed questions; I used more 'we' and other inclusive pronouns to reduce distance between myself and the learners; and when someone was off task instead of saying, 'Get on with your work, you should have written a full paragraph by now!' I'd ask, 'How are you getting on with the start of your story?' I tended to use language to be supportive rather than regulatory. In essence, I used more politeness markers to build relationships and connect. Contrastingly, at the start of my career I would have taken a more frustrated, distanced and regulatory approach when learners appeared to be off task. And crucially, at the outset of my teaching experience in a SEN school, I used the advice I was given by staff and worked with what I was told the learners were familiar with in terms of the school's reward (and sanction) systems. Did these work? For the most part, yes.

But what about connecting to enhance the actual supported and independent learning for these learners with varying degrees of autism? How was I going to support the neurodiverse learning needs of the group? One thing I found valuable was to think about the arrangement of the tables and use of space in the classroom. I changed the layout of the teaching areas of the room which helped me to maintain better face-to-face contact and communication with all learners. Also, a change in the layout of the teaching space made my movements during the lessons more efficient, a much more ergonomic process for movement you might say.

The central learning space was a large C shape with the students around the outside of the shape. I used a swivel chair with wheels and moved within the inside of the C and maintained a face-to-face connection when speaking to the individual learners rather than looking over a learner's shoulder when moving around the classroom. To me there is a major difference between standing over a learner and looking down at them or looking down at their work (there are chasms of added power dynamics with this) and being seated in front of them and basically being with them. I took advantage of changing the layout of the classroom. Yes, 'took advantage' because I knew that changing aspects of physical space in a classroom would not be possible in all places or spaces, but the change was about making better connections with my learners in this space.

MONITORING   ENVIRONMENT   SPACIAL PRESENCE

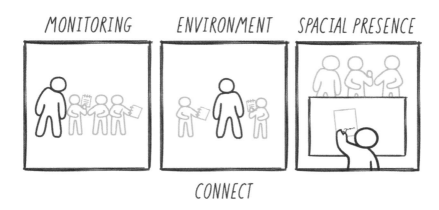

CONNECT

Another valuable thing was learning to write and master writing upside down on the tables … Writing on wipeable tables was a practice throughout the school, and yes there was the laborious task of cleaning tables at the end of lessons, but it was worth it! There were moments when individual learners also participated in writing on the table then looking up whilst speaking, and this speaking-and-writing took on its own rhythmic sequence.

For instance, I would use features of phonics and whole word recognition when supporting these learners with their spelling whilst writing on the table in front of the learner, and they were expected to participate in writing and learning to spell or scribe to support the organising of ideas for their written work. As simple as this may sound, I found looking at the learner and writing upside down made the communication and connecting easier on both sides. I could watch and begin to read their facial expressions, and they always seemed to watch, sometimes fascinated, as letters then words formed on the table in front of them.

How exactly did changing my teaching space and learning to write upside down help me to connect with my neurodiverse learners? I made the effort to adapt, and I tried something unusual and it happened to hold the attention and increase the concentration of learners. They knew it took some effort on my part, and crucially, they knew the effort was to support their individual learning.

SOCIAL MEDIA

Join the conversation by using the hashtag #myteachingroutine on social media. Share with other educators how you connect with your learners within the classroom. You can showcase your example through a photo, video, presentation slide or post.

CHAPTER 2
[DEMONSTRATE]

 Don't teach a learner to achieve for a day, show them how to achieve for life. - Mark Martin

OVERVIEW

THIS CHAPTER EXPLORES THE FOLLOWING IDEAS:

* DEMONSTRATING WHAT LEARNERS NEED TO DO THROUGH A LESSON WILL HELP TO INCREASE FOCUS AND MOTIVATION
* VISUALLY SEEING THE END GOAL HELPS TO INSPIRE LEARNERS TO ENVISION THEIR OUTCOMES
* SHOWCASING THE STARTING AND END POINT PROVIDES GREATER STRUCTURE FOR COMPLETION OF THE TASK
* DIFFERENTIATING THE LEVELS OF PROGRESS HELPS THE LEARNER TO UNDERSTAND THEIR JOURNEY

Selecting effective demonstrations, and knowing when and how to use them effectively can be a challenge. The power of demonstration helps to keep learners focused, motivated and informed, and that is true whether or not they are making progress in that part of the lesson activity or module. Demonstrations, or what some call modelling or providing clear examples of the stages or the outcome, are crucial. Demonstrations can be done in a variety of ways and by using different methods, but they need to be consistent and normalised for learners.

LESSON OBJECTIVES

A common form of demonstration is lesson objectives because it gives context and meaning to why we do certain things in our classroom. For many teachers across England, displaying the lesson objectives on the projector as soon as the learners enter the classroom is compulsory and part of the school's teaching and learning policy.

The three main domains of a lesson objective are:

- Cognitive domain – Academic capability
- Affective domain – Emotions, social and feelings
- Psychomotor domain – Manual and physical skills

Each domain is classified into levels of complexity and specificity. Benjamin Bloom and a group of educators devised accordingly a taxonomy of educational objectives (Bloom, 1956). This is where the term Bloom's Taxonomy originates and it has become the most widely applied method of classification. In 2001, Anderson and Krathwohl (2001) revised Bloom's taxonomy to Remember, Understand, Apply, Analyse, Evaluate and Create. The hierarchy defines each cognitive level from higher to lower order thinking. The aim is to help teachers build schemes of work that challenge learners' thinking and produce effective learning outcomes centred around knowledge, skills or attitude.

Teachers are encouraged to get learners to write the lesson objectives down, which has widely been criticised for wasting teaching time; but I think a positive aspect of writing down lesson objectives gives the class a moment of silence and focus, which helps the teacher to create a calm environment at the start of the lesson. Designing quality learning objectives that 'make sense' to learners requires good planning by the teacher and understanding of the scheme of work by the learners. It should allow learners to see where they are and what they need to do to get to the next level. This should be linked to the subject success criteria and exam framework where possible. This alignment prepares learners for exam success and meeting their academic targets. However to avoid this being a tick box exercise it's recommended that you explore evidence-based practice to make informed decisions when it comes to designing lesson objectives. I don't think it should be enforced through the school's learning policies, which makes the routine a burden. It's important to acknowledge that every learner interprets the lesson objectives differently: some are oblivious, frustrated or careless when objectives are not clear or are confusing; in turn this uncertainty will impact their attitude, behaviour and aspiration when it comes to completing the work. The lesson objectives need to be differentiated, achievable, relevant and acknowledged when learners have made progress. The All/Most/Some is sometimes not the best format to use when getting learners engaged and excited about the task they need to complete. Providing specific examples and clear demonstrations are powerful ways to broaden the learning objectives.

TAKING OWNERSHIP

Demonstration can be decentralised to give learners ownership and a sense of responsibility. Reminding learners on a regular basis to monitor their efforts is purposeful, and monitoring can take many forms. These approaches may include co-creating the lesson objectives with the learners by giving them a choice or selection of outcomes they would like to achieve by the end of the lesson. They can either ask their peers or teacher to hold them to account through the process. Another approach could be designing a progress tracker that allows learners to monitor their progress and performance. The tracker can be assessed by their peers, parents or teachers. Their termly grades can be added, or peer-to-peer reviewed. This form of self-monitoring takes time for learners to embrace because many learners are reliant on the teacher to provide an instant response to their progress and performance. You could add in some non-academic objectives in the process, which take into consideration the learners' mental health and wellbeing. To get learners on board, find some common ground, acknowledge and praise their efforts. This can be a great approach when starting a complex or difficult part of your course. In these situations reach for more demonstrations and examples for learners to understand the landscape. But don't assume they know how to navigate the content based on your lesson objectives or explanation solely.

SHARED GOALS AND CO-CREATION

Another form of demonstration is co-creation which encourages learners and teachers to become partners who each have a voice and stake in the lesson outcomes. This builds a partnership based on respect, reciprocity and shared responsibility (Cook-Sather et al., 2014). Co-creation provides an insight into learners' diverse worlds, where their background, culture and experiences intertwine. When considering 'inclusion' most teachers might use music, art, drama, icons or local stories to illuminate their demonstration. Although these items may be representative of the learners' interests and experiences, they may not reach the depths of who they are as individuals or inform teachers how to connect with them in an inclusive way. Teachers need to make space and room for learners to express their interests and experiences. The practical steps to making this happen could be to create a poll, survey or questionnaire on the VLE (Virtual Learning System) system to capture learners' thoughts and ideas. The teacher then can unpack the feedback and embed these connections into the content, pedagogy and/or marking criteria. By inviting learners to be a part of the lesson design it helps to make the demonstration and examples relevant. Although co-creation can be more work and take more time to execute, it makes the learning experience fun and exciting. The reason why co-creation doesn't happen a lot in schools is probably because of the time it takes to train teachers and learners, and it doesn't show a clear link to exam success; however, I would argue, co-creation creates a stronger bond between teacher and learner during the demonstration process.

CO-TEACHING

Learners can be an integral part of lesson demonstrations, by simply allowing them to take part.

• How much ownership do learners have in the content delivery?
• Do we give them enough opportunity to express themselves?

I ask myself these questions on a regular basis, and seek ways to get my learners involved at every opportunity available. Getting learners involved presents openings for equal opportunities for all learners, including the more reserved or introverted ones. When learners leave our institutions they need to have a range of soft skills that help them represent themselves in the outside world and become active citizens.

As highlighted in the previous chapter, education is much more than learners sitting and listening to their teachers for knowledge. It's about helping them to understand the world around them and being able to navigate different spaces. Using learners in the classroom (in roles equivalent to co-teachers) can enhance their confidence and information retention. This speaking and participation framework is another example of ways in which you can encourage and support oracy in your subject.

Learners as co-teachers

In order to get your learners trained to be co-teachers you will need to create a script or framework to support learners to explain their own work in a concise format, use the correct terminology and lexis, and use positive body language to present to their peers. Once the learners understand what is expected of them, the demonstrations can take many forms. Learners can use their previous work to showcase to peers and explain what they need to do in order to meet the lesson objectives and outcomes. Another option is to get learners to design a mini presentation on the keywords or technical terms they have learned. You can use a rotation system so all learners get an opportunity to demonstrate and to showcase their work.

Online demonstrations

With the rise of online teaching it can be a very passive experience for learners, however getting learners to be co-teachers will encourage active participation virtually. To do this learners can either do a three- to five-minute demonstration to their peers or they could pre-record their demonstration using a video recording of themselves. Also you could get learners to comment or generate questions on your or the co-learners' demonstration using the online chat tool. This keeps them involved and actively listening for keywords and technical terms. Co-teaching spaces like this will require time and patience because some learners may resist or refuse to engage in the process. You could get older groups or higher-ed learners to role model to your younger learners.

INCLUSIVE TEACHING

Demonstrating to the classwork without thinking about inclusion may instantly alienate a range of learners. The relationship between inclusivity and what is being demonstrated is closely linked. Teachers are normally encouraged within their lesson plan to design interventions for special educational needs learners. Catering for different needs can be a challenge, but teachers that design lessons with special educational needs and disabilities at their core enable all learners irrespective of their circumstances to enjoy the fullest possible learning experience.

Different needs

Understanding autism, dyslexia and dyspraxia as well as learners with ADHD, Tourette's syndrome and speech, language and communication difficulties helps you to be a mindful and effective educator. These needs illustrate that no learner is the same and we should value learners that have different kinds of minds. This highlights a positive challenge that teachers face when it comes to developing teaching materials and using technology.

Implementation and resources

When presenting, the presentation slides need to be clear, concise and easy to follow. Also, many learners with educational needs often attribute difficulties with learning to not having access to handouts or class notes during or after lessons; this can be alleviated by working with teaching assistants and one-to-one support staff beforehand. Additionally, uploading class materials for the whole school term on the school's VLE and using a scheduled release for learners and their support staff is a way to help such learners. This gives learners the opportunity to access the content before and after the lesson. I noticed that learners would use my class notes on their digital devices as I started to explain and demonstrate the lesson objectives. I think this helped them to manage the pace of the lesson by either going back to slides to process the information or write down keywords. I also made sure for some learners that I printed out the learning materials so they have a physical copy if needed. Another thing that I have found effective is to provide learners at the beginning of the lesson with a list of technical terms, glossaries and further reading materials.

Social emotional needs and mindfulness

Inclusive teaching goes beyond the content and pedagogy, focusing on the very real social, emotional and cognitive demands of learning. When demonstrating class materials it's important teachers are aware that their approach and style can trigger stresses, anxiety or knock learners confidence. It requires teachers to understand and embrace mindfulness and empathy to those around them. According to the Merriam-Webster Dictionary, mindfulness is 'the practice of maintaining a non-judgmental state of heightened or complete awareness of one's thoughts, emotions, or experiences on a moment-to-moment basis'. Jon Kabat-Zinn, a renowned thought leader in this space, states that mindfulness is the practice of non-judgemental awareness in the present moment and non-reactive, non-judgemental and open-hearted observation (Kabat-Zinn, 1994). Mindfulness can alleviate learners' stress and anxiety (Viafora et al., 2015).

According to Peerayuth Charoensukmongkol, mindfulness breeds emotional intelligence in three ways:

1.   It improves your ability to comprehend your own emotions
2.   It helps you learn how to recognise the emotions of other people around you
3.   It strengthens your ability to govern and control your emotions

Peerayuth's research suggests that mindfulness can improve your ability to use your emotions effectively, through determining which emotions are beneficial for certain situations (Charoensukmongkol, 2014). Understanding these dynamics will significantly help teachers when demonstrating new content and topics to the class.

Remote learning

Another area of inclusive teaching is remote learning; demonstrating work online is not the same as demonstrating work in person. The pressure to remain focused by looking at a screen can take its toll and asking for help is not as rapid as being in a classroom. Despite this, according to Kate Lister, Jane Seale and Chris Douce, distance learners disclose mental health issues at a higher rate than in-school learners (Lister et al., 2021). Before demonstrating the content, check in on learners to see how they are coping with their workload and whether they need any additional support. Creating a supportive, empathetic learning environment on and offline is what I predict will be a key feature for remote learning.

ALIGNING TEACHING FOR CONSTRUCTING LEARNING

Over the years there has been much discourse on the building blocks to learning and demonstrating what learners need to learn. For example the structure of the Observed Learning Outcome (solo) taxonomy classifies the learning outcomes in terms of their complexity. In comparison, constructive alignment is about defining the learning outcomes and aligning them with teaching and assessment strategies (Biggs, 1999). There is no perfect formula to constructing learning because there are different contexts and demands from education systems and schools. Showing the grade criteria in my lesson plans and displaying them up on the board before learners entered the classroom seemed to be the norm for every lesson. When I observed other teachers they seemed to follow the same method of making sure the grade criteria were visible for all learners. But if you asked the learners whether they know if they have completed a task to a satisfactory standard, the majority thought that the completion of the task was the ultimate goal. However, Biggs' constructing learning is about getting learners to construct meaning by interpreting the grade criteria in the context of their own experiences and prior knowledge. To help learners to digest or recall new information effectively, the new information needs to be organised and interpreted following a framework or concept, which is normally known as a schema. The constructivism view is to explore what learners already know, so that new knowledge can be related to the existing schemas. This is where a teacher's culture capital and connection is paramount, because schemas can be cultural. Lev Vygotsky (1978: 57) suggested that,

> Every function in the learners' cultural development appears twice: first, on the social level and, later on, on the individual level; first, between people interpsychological and then inside the learner intrapsychological.

The learners use their social and cultural compass to see whether the teacher has their best interest in mind. Learners will consciously read their teachers by the way they make them feel during the lesson. Based on the teachers' responses, interactions and acknowledgement learners will decide to connect or disconnect. Teachers shouldn't assume they understand their learners until they make an effort to listen and understand their lived experiences. It's better to engage learners by giving them space to express themselves with new ideas and skills without dismissing their efforts. Use these opportunities to incorporate their insights into your lessons and demonstrate how they can enhance their skills against the lesson objectives. This will develop learners' confidence, create memorable moments and opportunities to build on the hidden skill sets they bring to school everyday.

USING VISUAL AIDS

Visual aids can be used in demonstrating what learners need to learn. The idea that making information visual for learners is ideal for engagement and holding their attention. Images are not solely shapes and graphics they can take many forms, from spatial awareness, and include different colours and tones, brightness and contrast and font variations. Visual images help to communicate, exchange ideas and unpack new information. The rise of the internet has made access to images easier for teachers to use in the classroom and teaching materials. Using images as visual learning aids is all about seeing things in order to learn them. It helps to summarise content into smaller chunks, which is more comprehensible than text-based explanations or audio alone. With the rise of presentation tools and software functionality it's easier than ever to animate and present images in new and exciting ways, from fading in images one at a time to showing animated sequences of content. Combining technology and the images provides a new dimension to simplify complex topics into visual images that learners can understand. However teachers can complicate the process by using lots of images, images over text, vibrant colours and distracting animations. This can be very confusing for individuals who are colour blind, dyslexic or autistic so it's imperative inclusive design features (i.e. clear font, text and pale backgrounds) are taken into consideration when using visual learning to demonstrate lesson content and objectives.

Using images to scaffold or model learning can be an effective visual aid to inspire and motivate learners. You can use digital images or freehand images on the board to either showcase what you want your learners to achieve or milestones for them to reach at key stages in the learning. You can also use visual images to model what levels or standards look like so learners understand what they need to do. Modelling good practice helps to encourage the class to have a clear focus and helps the learner to understand when a milestone has been reached. The images may not lead the learners to the answers but give them an idea of what is possible and their own journey of discovery. You can be very creative in what images you use to show the development and progress of the lesson activities. The aim is to avoid explaining too much knowledge and instructions, which may lead to learners losing focus and being confused about what they need to learn. Over-talking and/or over-imaging does not support good demonstrations or modelling. I have used images to model learning in a Year 10 computer science lesson, such as the plant diagram shown in the figure below, which breaks down the stages of lesson completion.

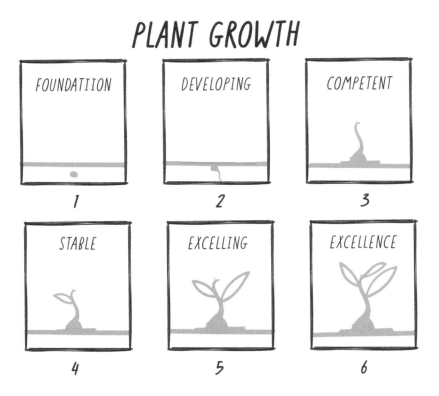

The seed represents the foundation level (1), a sprouting plant represents a stable level (4), and a flourishing plant represents the excelling level (6). The example showed clarity, differentiation and workflow, which was important for learners of different abilities. Not all learners will reach the excelling level but they have the opportunity to see the stages of progression. The power of using images to showcase progression helps the learner to track and monitor their efforts. It keeps the process transparent and easy to follow. Instead of using numbers or sentences you can use images across the presentation slides and activity sheets to subtly show learners where they are at with their learning.

ACTIVE LEARNING USING VISUAL AND AUDIO AIDS

There are different forms of demonstrating what learners need to know and what they are supposed to achieve by the end of the lesson. Some teachers may use verbal instructions, handouts, presentation slides or pre-recorded materials to assist with conveying their expectations. Learners will either be passive or active depending on the approach and style the teacher decides to use. Passive learning is when the learner takes in information from the teacher or instructional materials without overtly doing anything else. The teacher may use audio and visual aids to settle the class, promote active listening and build confidence in the learners before they commence the main activity. The drawbacks are when learners become bored, distracted or confused, which creates an additional challenge for the teacher. Active learning is when the learner participates in the demonstration process in the form of discussion, questioning, writing down notes, or showcasing their prior skills or knowledge. It enforces full engagement from the learner as opposed to just replicating and regurgitating the information given. The thing to consider with active learning during a demonstration is time keeping, to keep learners focused and engaged.

Background

Over the years teachers have started to introduce videos and audio into their lessons to demonstrate activities and learning outcomes. The use of interactive multimedia, audio/video tutorials and asynchronous content has taken centre stage in the discourse around educational technology. You can now narrate presentation slides, explain concepts through audio, answer learners' questions with voice notes and demonstrate how to solve subject content through videos. The content can then be uploaded on the VLE platform for learners to access remotely. The pandemic has organically endorsed asynchronous learning allowing learners to learn at their own pace and contribute to discussions by recording their answers via audio or video.

STRUCTURING YOUR PRESENTATION SLIDE FOR BETTER ENGAGEMENT

As an edtech specialist it would be a crime if I didn't mention a few ideas on how you can use presentation slides to increase engagement during the demonstrating part of the lesson. The best presentations are clear and easy to follow because they are not cluttered with unnecessary information.

Heading

Adding an action word as a title for each slide keeps the learners alert, for example calling a slide 'demonstration' gets straight to the point and everyone is clear with the process.

Main body and dual coding

The main body of the slide can have equal weight in text (verbal communication) and image (non-verbal processing), which is known as the dual coding theory. Allan Paivio coined the theory when he identified that our memory has two channels, which focus on visual and verbal stimuli. Whilst our memory stores them separately, the words and images are linked, which makes retrieval easier when prompted. Paivio states, 'Human cognition is unique in that it has become specialised for dealing simultaneously with language and with nonverbal objects and events' (Paivio, 1990: p53). When the word or image is used it can stimulate the learner to retrieve the necessary information. Using dual coding in your demonstrations will help to reduce the learners' cognitive load, allowing them to focus on the key items. I normally insert an image on the slide of what learners need to achieve and add bullet points of technical or keywords to help them retain the information.

Testing learners

To ensure learners have grasped the demonstration I would display a similar slide during the lesson but leave out some elements and test them on their thought process. On many occasions when I thought learners had understood the demonstration, testing them revealed they got some of the concepts mixed up. Demonstrating is a continual process that can be used throughout the lesson. As mentioned in the previous section, you can get your learners involved by getting them to design their own dual code materials or presentation slides demonstrating their work.

CLASSROOM EXPERIENCE

In the GCSE computer science scheme of work there is a section on ethical, legal and environmental impacts of digital technology. The learners need to understand how technology affects people's daily lives. The topic is very broad but learners need to know how to apply the keywords (ethical, legal, environmental and culture) to any topic discussed. For example, if the topic was on facial recognition they would need to apply the keywords to the matter. I needed to ensure learners had understood the keywords and knew how to apply them to different contexts. Instead of teaching the keywords I provided a glossary and got them to apply their experiences to them. The majority had shouted out their lived experience using their mobile phones – from being scammed to fake influencers. I was then able to use their examples to demonstrate how the keywords could be applied and what makes a good sentence construction. The engagement for activity significantly improved and learners knew exactly what they needed to do. During this activity learners controlled some areas of choice and partnered with me to make the topic come alive.

REFLECTION

Experience has taught me that in every scheme of work there is an opportunity to give learners a stake in the design and delivery. This is a negotiated space for learning, where learners play a pivotal role in shaping the teaching and learning. I guess the fear for many teachers is letting go, or not having enough time to prepare; or even a sense of losing their status as an authoritative figure in the classroom. There have been many occasions where learners spend a whole weekend looking at YouTube and come to lessons with advanced knowledge that I wasn't taught in my degree or on my teaching course. Instead of shutting them down, I reflect on where I could add those skills and insights into my lesson activities for a greater variety of demonstrations. This sharing does not only benefit teachers but all participants since there is reciprocity and respect for innovative ideas that benefit both teacher and learner(s) as they learn from each other.

 REFLECTION QUESTIONS

- **When planning work for your learners to complete for skill building or assessment, do you have examples of what a poor, a good or an outstanding outcome, for instance, looks like?**
- **Also do you use help guides or frameworks to help them transition to the next level?**
- **Do we need to show the learner the destination/end goal, or should they just follow instructions as we take them on a journey through the content?**
- **How should those demonstrations be delivered?**
- **When could those demonstrations be used most effectively?**

DEMONSTRATION IN THE REAL WORLD

You could think of a demonstration as a football tactic being used on a flipboard to explain to players what the manager wants them to do against the opposing team. There is no doubt that a football manager has to be clear when explaining match tactics with his or her players. One style would be to stand in front of the players and use body movements to demonstrate what the players should be doing on the field; Manchester City's Pep Gurdiola is known for this. Without visualising what the manager is trying to convey to the players it could be difficult to understand and know what they are really supposed to do. However, by visualising the tactics through using a flipboard with an outline of a pitch and players occupying certain spaces on the field, the manager can use shapes and images on the board to make the tactics easier to follow. The manager could then create a dialogue with the players to check if they understand his demonstrations and provide space for players to give their own suggestions. The overall goal would be to ensure all parties understand their role and they are on the same page.

The football manager analogy is similar to a teacher's objective to get learners to understand what they are expected to achieve during the lesson. You may not be able to use fields and arrows but you can model what learners need to achieve; the modelling examples can be broken down into stages and managed into chunks so that learners can access the information and know when they are making progress.

HINTS & TIPS

- Avoid using lots of text in your presentations
- Use images to show progression
- Use demonstrations to show the endless possibilities
- Get learners to demonstrate their own understanding

WHEN CONNECT AND DEMONSTRATE COME TOGETHER

In addition, when it comes to assimilating a technical word such as 'algorithms' into the learner's own cultural schema and using these schemas to make sense of the technical word, I normally provide an everyday example of the technical word and then see if learners have their own example of the word. The majority of the time learners could verbally connect their technical words to their everyday lives. However, when I directed them to write the technical words into their own paragraphs or use them in an exam question, some learners struggled. The teacher's ability to provide rich context to technical words helps the learner to assimilate the information into their relevant schema. If the information is weak or unclear then the learners develop a poor foundation to build on. It's imperative that the subject knowledge, relationships, real world experiences and blind spots are factored in when it comes to constructing a good lesson.

CLASSROOM EXPERIENCE

In my Key Stage 3 ICT classes, I decided to record the lesson objectives, the different targets for the lesson, the different levels of attainment in the unit, and recapped the learning from previous lessons. I wanted to ensure learners who had missed lessons or wanted to revisit the work had the opportunity to do so in their own time. For learners that were not able to access the content at home, the ICT department organised weekly after-school clubs. When I checked the analytics on the VLE, to my surprise the interaction with the content was good.

The challenge

The challenge I had was consistency, ensuring every week I recorded myself explaining the lesson content. Also having pre-recorded instructions or demonstrations helped save time, and reduced this aspect of my workload. One advantage here is that you avoid having to repeat the same or even similar instructions several times. You may need to train and support learners for several lessons before they get comfortable with these methods of working.

HINTS & TIPS

1. **Use stock photos for human images**
2. **Use icon packs for graphics and illustrations**
3. **Audio record on your digital device**
4. **Prepare 30-second lesson objectives**

PERSONAL EXPERIENCE

Setting the scene for learners to understand the stages of the lessons' goals can be a challenging experience because you are trying to show them the big picture based on your style and approach. Whether they can interpret or translate your explanation of this is the big question.

Initial teacher training

In our teacher training we are taught to generate lesson objectives for each lesson. These are then displayed on a whiteboard or projector at the start of the lesson. The lesson objectives are normally broken down into levels of theoretical and practical application, and that is usually subject dependent. Depending on the topic, the lesson objectives are accompanied by teacher-led tutorials or demonstrations to provide the learner with greater guidance and understanding.

LESSON OBSERVATIONS

When observing other teachers, I noticed lesson demonstrations had taken many forms, from a handout, to teacher led or learner led. The confident teachers would allow their learners to lead from the front, whereas some less confident teachers would lead the demonstration whilst managing the conduct of the class. I have found the real aim of using demonstrations, highlighted tasks or learning outcomes at the start of the lesson is to get learners to think about managing their progress, and then work independently towards their levels by using the lessons objectives, or using any signposted information as a road map through the lesson.

REFLECTION

In the past, once I had demonstrated the lesson objectives, I normally assumed learners knew what they had to do, and what a good standard of work would look like. The lesson demonstrations helped me in particular to plan and give me a direction for my lessons; but at times I found that particular demonstrations didn't have the same impact for the learners.

The majority of times, learners would produce work they thought met the standard but weren't sure on which objective they had completed. On many occasions when testing learners' understanding of the levels through questioning they couldn't identify where they were making progress.

CLASSROOM EXPERIENCE

In my Year 7 ICT lesson learners could tell me the acronym RAM stood for Read Only Memory, and with that they could tell me some technical terms of RAM, i.e. volatile, temporary and dynamic. However, to achieve a higher level my learners needed to be able to explain RAM in greater detail, such as how it is used in the real world; and this was missing from their written answers. In order to stretch my learners' thinking and understanding I devised a framework which helped the learners to define the acronym and write down its benefits.

I then levelled the framework:

Foundation – Define RAM acronym

Stable – Provide a definition of RAM with technical terms

Excelling – List several benefits of RAM using technical terms

I found greater success in facilitating learning when I started to demonstrate what these levels looked like, especially by using visual examples, and being specific on the amount of words required to complete each statement. The learners soon grasped that if they got stuck or struggled they could use the help guide that I provided. This guide included a range of colours and steps to progress through, and with the colour guide the learner was able to reach the next stage of their learning progression. In my Year 11 computer science class my learners struggled to write in full sentences when explaining technical concepts. So I used a level descriptor to show what a good explanation looked like. If they wrote two to three lines without any technical terms the level descriptor would indicate that the piece of work was stable; however, if they added a few more lines with technical words that would significantly improve the attainment in their work. The level descriptor was used as a support to get my learners not to rush through the work but take their time and think about the content of their work. I realised the power of demonstration and being specific in what you want the learners to produce or reach during a lesson.

 REFLECTION QUESTIONS

- Are you conscious of when your learners are in an active or passive state?
- How do you include all learners within the demonstration?
- Are you conscious of the time you take to lead a demonstration?
- How do you know your learners have understood your demonstration?

ANOTHER TEACHER'S EXPERIENCE: KATHERINE MCLOUGHLIN (HEAD OF ENGLISH – SECONDARY SCHOOL)

One of the first pieces of advice I give to any teacher I'm mentoring or supporting is to try writing out end-point answers themselves before any planning or teaching takes place. For me, as an English teacher, this means writing out descriptive prose paragraphs, short stories, or essays. This was one of the steepest learning curves I went through as an NQT (or more realistically as an RQT). In some ways this becomes a bit of a Blue-Peter-esque 'here's one I made earlier' moment: a clear text to demonstrate as an outcome to the given task. Demonstration isn't simply a way to model to students what you want them to aim towards (though this is an important element of demonstration). I also view accurate demonstration as a key route to building confidence. Demonstration is also a process. It helps me to create personal confidence in my own knowledge and teaching by acting as a route to continuous mastery of knowledge – both at a subject and specification level. Carefully writing my own answers also increased my ability to articulate what I actually wanted students to achieve. For my students, I feel it helps to develop their respect and confidence in me as a practitioner. They become more confident that I am the expert in the room. Demonstration also acts as a guiding route for my ongoing planning. When writing any answer, I force myself to pause and consider the steps that I'm actually taking. It is this reflection on the different steps that allows me to identify what my lessons need to be focused on. These steps range from how to embed evidence into an analytical paragraph, or even how to vary sentence starts in prose writing. The way I use demonstration in class has evolved over my time as a teacher. Initially I aimed to have examples ready to show my classes. These very much acted as polished finished pieces, rather than necessarily allowing students themselves to be involved in the demonstration. In some ways this works well as a route to giving an idealised end point. For more able students (or as a route to revision after initial teaching) this can be an effective way to allow students to break down the steps I've used to create a piece of writing. On further reflection on my practice, I began to realise that focusing merely on the final result had the potential to be both intimidating and make the students themselves quite passive in their learning. Now I've learnt that demonstration requires a mixture of the finished product and the process itself. This has meant that I've increasingly used my time in lessons to actively demonstrate writing in front of my students, pausing between different steps to both explain my thought process and to challenge students to explain what they believe I need to do next. Increasingly, this has relied on different forms of technology in the classroom.

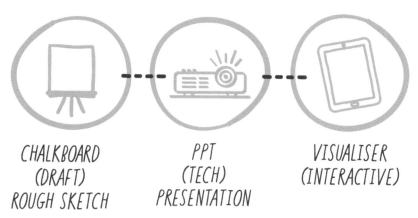

CHALKBOARD
(DRAFT)
ROUGH SKETCH

PPT
(TECH)
PRESENTATION

VISUALISER
(INTERACTIVE)

My initial teaching on my PGCE was using whiteboards and chalkboards, which presented pretty obvious limitations for demonstration in terms of board space. This evolved into typing and colour coding using PowerPoints. More recently I've been able to use a visualiser (a digital version of an OHP) that makes the whole process feel more natural. Students can see me needing to go back and physically cross out the errors or the sentences I've decided I need to change. The use of visualisers in my classroom has enabled me to also update my demonstration of the relevant mark scheme. I've been able to 'live' mark pieces of work in front of classes, with all seeing exactly what I'm highlighting as achievement and what needs to be corrected. As my teaching moves towards greater focus on student reflection and peer assessment, this style of demonstration has proved invaluable as a way to model the processes they should also be following.

SOCIAL MEDIA

Join the conversation by using the hashtag #myteachingroutine on social media. Share with other educators how you demonstrate what learners need to know in your lessons. You can showcase your example through a photo, video, presentation slide or post.

CHAPTER 3
[ACTIVATE]

 Timing is everything in teaching; the influential educators know when to start, stop and pause. They listen to the heartbeat of the classroom before a decision is made. - Mark Martin

OVERVIEW

THIS CHAPTER EXPLORES THE FOLLOWING IDEAS:

* TIMING IS EVERYTHING WHEN IT COMES TO TEACHING
* LEARNERS FAILING TO UNDERSTAND INSTRUCTIONS CAN WASTE VALUABLE CLASSROOM TIME AND LEAD TO LOW LEVEL DISRUPTIONS
* CHECKING FOR UNDERSTANDING OF THE INSTRUCTIONS LEADS TO BETTER OUTCOMES
* CLEAR INSTRUCTIONS PRODUCE BETTER FOCUS AND EFFORT
* REPETITION OF INSTRUCTIONS CAN LEAD TO SPOON FEEDING

In essence, activating in my teaching routine means to trigger, set off, or energise the learners to engage with the main activity or purpose of the lesson; and this usually happens after a connection is made between the teacher and the learners as discussed in the preceding chapters. What I have labelled 'activating the lesson' is knowing when it is the right time for learners to commence the main activity or activities as independently as possible.

NOT ACTIVATING THE LESSON

It's very easy as a teacher not to activate the lesson, because you want to get all learners to have the same understanding. As a result the teacher's talk time significantly increases because you are having to repeat yourself, which might create levels of anxiety, frustration and a loss of time. This can potentially lead to losing the class's concentration and low level disruption. My best advice would be to give the learners enough confidence to start the task and then immediately activate the lesson. Then attend to those learners that struggled to understand what they needed to do. You can also pair learners who did understand the instructions with learners finding it difficult to activitate their learning. Once all learners have started the task you can select learners at random points of the lesson to check their understanding of the given task. In real terms, it is difficult to know exactly what learners are getting out of the lesson instructions unless you enquire.

WHEN TO START THE LESSON

Before the learners start the main learning task the teacher should offer support, direction, information and the materials to aid learning, so that learners feel confident about what they need to do or achieve in the various stages of the lesson. The teacher might use questioning, low stake testing or open dialogue to ensure learners understand what to do throughout the main activity. Based on the learners' response and feedback, the teacher might spend extra time going through the content and instructions. A common mistake that many teachers make is they spend too much time explaining the activity, spoon feeding or being too hands on and not allowing the learners to start the task independently. As a result, learners become over-dependent on the teacher. It is important to avoid learners becoming over-reliant on their teachers; they need to step back and initiate the learning.

A COMMON MISTAKE

Another common mistake is when teachers try to centralise the steps so all the class has to move at the same pace through the activities. This is a difficult thing to do because trying to sync their learning to match your tempo can lead to learners struggling to keep up with your teaching. Sometimes it's better to decentralise the classroom by allowing learners to commence the task when they are ready and confident. This approach enables you to become the facilitator or coach that gives guidance on the side, instead of trying to hold everyone's attention in the classroom. If you are having to do this online, using the breakout room function will provide learners the option to either listen to the keynote of the lesson or join a room and commence the task. Also, as mentioned in the previous chapter, you could record video clips for learners giving them advice or support once they have completed a particular task. The asynchronous approach is becoming popular in schools because it provides the option to revisit the teacher's instructions and explanations.

PRIOR KNOWLEDGE AND ELICITING

The teacher can also build on learners' existing knowledge or experiences. This knowledge can be activated and used constructively when commencing the main task. This approach is called eliciting, and it encourages the learner to explore what they know about a subject and begin building on the current information being presented. Eliciting is not limited to the learners' prior knowledge; their current experiences can elicit new ideas, feelings, meanings, situations, associations and memories. When we use eliciting in activating the learning, we ask learners questions or give cues to get them to explain what they know about the subject rather than the teacher giving the explanation. Learners are also given prompts, associations and reminders in order to jog their memories. This guided discovery leads to better understanding and more inclusive learning, which makes information more memorable and fun. One thing to consider is whether the learners lack knowledge or are not confident to reveal their prior knowledge. The teacher will need to create opportunities for learners to engage through providing extra materials or guidance.

THE RIGHT TIME TO START THE MAIN TASK

There are many ways to start a lesson and get learners engaged in the class activities. Here are a few approaches you can take:

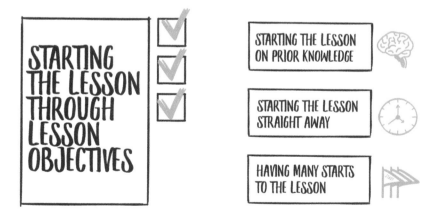

Starting the lesson through lesson objectives

Once the teacher has explained the lesson objectives, scheme of work and instructions for the activity, then the learners commence the task. This approach is content driven and allows the learner to start the task once they have enough guidance to activate the lesson. To keep learners on task you might want to get them involved through explaining to peers what they need to achieve.

Starting the lesson based on prior knowledge

Teachers can start the lesson if they feel learners have prior knowledge from previous lessons or experiences to commence the task. The teacher may support learners with learning materials and one-to-one guidance. Also the teacher might check learners' knowledge by asking a series of questions and getting learners to assess their peers' progress.

Starting the lesson straight away

Teachers can activate the lesson straight away and assist learners as they commence the task. This requires extra bandwidth and capacity to ensure every learner is on task and knows what they are doing individually. To keep learners on task the teacher might leave the learning objectives on the board, accompanied by learning materials such as handouts. This approach can descend into chaos if all the learners start to go off task, or complete the work before others.

Having many starts to lessons

Teachers can have multiple starts to a lesson if it's broken down into small parts. The way this is done is by differentiating the learning activities and allowing certain learners to commence tasks independently. This approach can foster greater collaboration amongst learners and decentralise the classroom.

In summary, there is no correct way to start the lesson but your approach needs to be direct, intentional, purpose driven, timed and clinical. The difficulties may be encountered when teachers are not clear or in control of how they want the lesson to be activated.

INSTRUCTIONS

When activating a lesson teachers provide a range of different instructions for learners to digest and follow. Joyce et al. (2003) describe four categories of models of instruction:

- Behavioural systems
- Information processing
- Personal development
- Social interaction

These models summarise the vast majority of instructional methods we use in a classroom. The instruction of information processing is what teachers are mainly focused on to get learners to start the work. However, depending on your learners you may be required to raise morale with instructions around personal development and create boundaries with behaviour systems.

Personalised instructions

Helping your learners understand where they are at and what they need to do requires a personal dialogue with clear instructions. In a normal class setting it can be difficult to speak to every learner at the start of the activity, unless you pre-record the message and send it to them digitally. Then the next phase is to establish how well the learner has interpreted the instructions to independently proceed with classwork.

Data-centred instructions

Using pre-existing data on what instructions should be given to learners can be effective in meeting their needs. These data can be obtained through testing or tracking progress. The data provides the teacher with an holistic view on what learners have understood and what concepts need to be further explored. An example of a data instruction is the following:

> Learner A: the data has indicated you are 3 marks away from grade A. In order to reach your goal you will need to start this activity and produce 5 benefits and limitations.

FRAMEWORK

Each lesson activity should normally come with a framework or guide to steer the learner through the instruction or the particular step that they need to complete. The framework could be an exemplar of the activity or an extra breakdown of the concepts. The aim is to give enough support without providing the answer to the learner. In my model of teaching and learning the aim is for the teacher to empower the learner as much as possible, by encouraging the learner to draw out knowledge from a text, and by this I mean you as a teacher will be taking the learner down the path of active learning, rather than pouring in knowledge and causing passive learning where there is an opportunity and a purposeful activity to encourage independent learning. Let us be clear here: there will be times when the so-called knowledge pouring will prove the more useful and that will be dependent on a range of factors; but for the activate stage of this teaching and learning model, and I repeat, providing enough support without providing the answer helps your learners to be challenged at this stage, and other stages of their learning. I think that is healthy!

Another approach is to get learners who understand the framework to explain it to their peers. This is a powerful approach because this gets learners to verbally explain their understanding to their peers, which deepens their knowledge. The learner has to attempt to grasp the activity, choose words and prosodic features to communicate to the listener, and use time to deliver the communication.

This aids oracy. However, setting up the groups, the seating plans, etc. are also crucial – as mentioned in the chapter on the connect stage of the model. The teacher providing the answer should be the last resort that a learner should seek when they are unclear about the activity. Building resilience in learners is an important part of activating lessons – where normally they would depend on the teacher to steer them through the activities. Frameworks can take a lot of time to produce and can become outdated very quickly; you may want to think about developing a hybrid model that can be accessed on and offline and which might help to make the material easy to maintain. Another approach could be to store the contents in a wiki format, which will help to develop a collaborative environment where learners could contribute to the development of the framework. However, another factor to take into consideration is the framework can also quickly become redundant if the learner doesn't see it as useful or they don't know how to apply it to their learning. The teacher will need to demonstrate to learners how to access the guide for low and high usage.

REUSABLE CHECKLIST

A checklist is different from the framework explored in the previous section because the latter is a resource that learners can refer to when they need guidance with their learning. The checklist enables the learner to tick off what they have achieved and what they have outstanding that they have yet to achieve. Checklisting is nothing new in teaching and learning; it comes down to how we as teachers use it in the classroom, and whether learners see its value.

How many times have we heard, 'I didn't know I had to do that…' or 'I forgot to do that part of the work…'?

What I call checklisting is an effective way of encouraging learners to take ownership of their learning because this aids learners to be in charge of self-assessing their progress. The checklist helps the teacher at a glance to note whether the learner has understood the instructions and made an effort to progress. The checklist can be a range of milestones or a set of questions that help to monitor whether the learners have completed the given task. The set of questions should be clear and minimal because the lesson objective would have stated in detail what the learners need to cover; and a checklist should complement the lesson objective. The aim of the checklist is to prevent learners forgetting where they left off, skipping tasks or rushing through tasks without understanding the journey or even the lesson activity.

Some checklists can be printed out on paper or programmed on an online platform which automates the feedback for the learner. You could get your learners to create their own checklist to measure their own effort and performance. This might take a lesson in itself to design and implement for learners to follow at the start of an activity, unit, or module of work.

The best checklist I created in my computer science lesson asked learners several questions:

- Have you written two lines for your definition?
- Have you provided a point and explanation, or did you use any technical terms? If so, underline them.
- Could you explain the concept without looking at your textbook?
- How is this concept used in the real world?

THE GLOSSARY

Another thing that I have found useful is to provide a glossary with the steps so learners can quickly refer to any key or technical words. When learners are completing the steps you will need to probe with tailored questions to check whether they are acknowledging their progress through the steps. It's important learners understand their learning journey rather than the destination, which is mostly centred around the answers. As mentioned in the previous chapter you could get learners to co-create the steps with you or provide multiple steps so there isn't a linear pathway – instead learners have to choose their own route to succeed.

STRUCTURED LEARNING STEPS

When activating the main activity, the information you provide to learners can be broken down into steps. Each step understood and completed helps the learner move on to the next step which is more challenging, or to consolidate the current learning. In order to keep the steps captivating one thing you can do is to display them on the board or screen, print them out, or upload them on the VLE.

EXTRA SUPPORT

Each step should come with some extra resources or added teacher input/assistance so learners can continue to climb the steps independently. If the steps are timed and come with a framework then it helps to encourage self-regulation. Some might label these extension activities which are given to learners who complete all the steps or want to be challenged at a higher level. Contrastingly, on occasion some learners may get stuck on a step or not fully understand what they need to do. To avoid these learners losing enthusiasm, verbal feedback or a series of supporting questions on the topic or concept under discussion can be used to encourage the learner to think further and progressively about the step so they can move on with their learning.

 HINTS & TIPS

1.   **On your presentation slide add an image to indicate when learners should commence the activity**
2.   **Allow learners to activate their work, once they have confirmed they have read the lesson materials**
3.   **Pair learners and allow them to activate each other's work based on two or three questions you have created to test learners' knowledge on what they need to do**

CLASS EXPERIENCE

A few years ago I introduced a framework into my computer science lessons to support low and high ability learners. When learners got stuck I would point them towards the framework to support their learning. I had noticed the learners were used to depending on me to guide their learning. But over a period of several lessons of pointing learners towards the framework when they got stuck, I would see them independently referring to the guide without any prompting or assistance. I realised that I had finally got them to use the framework when they became stuck or were struggling with aspects of their learning. The takeaway from using the framework was to regularly remind learners to use it in and out of the lesson.

 REFLECTION QUESTIONS

- **When is the right time to start a lesson activity?**
- **Do you wait for all learners to grasp the concepts before you let them commence the activity?**
- **Do you check their understanding and let them start the activity and support those that need extra help?**
- **Are you actively listening to learners' remarks and feedback when they start the task?**
- **If you have started to activate and the majority of learners are off task what do you do?**

TIME MANAGEMENT

In teaching you are given a specific amount of time to deliver a scheme of work over several months. In this time you are required to cover a specific amount of content and modules. The desired outcome is learners are prepared for their exams, project submissions or completion of modules. In order for teachers to meet these expectations, all stakeholders need to be informed of the time pressures.

There are several ways you can introduce time management into your lessons: you could display a countdown timer on the board so there is a clear reference point and learners know how much time they have – similar to a public examination. You could provide learners with a checklist of what they should be able to complete within the timeframe you have set. At the end you could get learners to reflect on whether they were able to complete the task in the timeframe you had set for them. You could also adopt the discreet method where you do not mention you are timing the activities to the learner. You could monitor the time and move onto the next activity using your watch or digital device. This approach would avoid putting any unnecessary pressure or anxiety on your learners or, most importantly, yourself. You could get learners to manage their own time and show them when it is the right time to transition into the next activity. You could provide criteria that learners would need to review before they commence the activity. You could use the eliciting technique to probe their understanding and root out any misconceptions throughout the lesson.

You will need to do this over several lessons for learners to adopt time management techniques but it will enable you to start the main activity with learners taking responsibility for their own learning.

DOCTORS' EXPERIENCE

Activating sometimes involves listening and looking out for signs (i.e. body language, tone, attitude, engagement, etc.), then responding accordingly to those indicators. Doctors have a similar role, because they need enough information from the patient to activate the best treatment and solution for the patient's condition. However doctors do get it wrong because they may stick to training manuals which may overlook the red flags and signs that the patient is trying to express to them. To reduce this problem doctors use prompt questions to further understand the patient's condition, and they will record things disclosed and not disclosed by the patient. Their active listening skills, which include verbal and nonverbal communication, will provide them with more information in understanding the patient's issue and symptoms. They may have access to the patient's medical records, be able to check family history, consult specialists, receive advice from other doctors, arrange several meetings with patients, and try different treatments and tests. Also, doctors need to have lots of empathy, compassion and understanding beyond the medical world. They also need to avoid being biased or confrontational, maintain high professional standards and most importantly, allow patients to tell their story. These characteristics are very similar traits to those teachers need in helping their learners reach their full potential. The probing that doctors do to find out what is wrong with their patient is comparable to what teachers need to do when supporting learners. Teachers need to have empathy, compassion and understanding in order to provide learners with a fair and equitable learning experience.

BENEATH THE SURFACE

The Anger Iceberg was first coined by the Gottman Institute, a team of researchers led by psychologists John and Julie Gottman. Their mission is to help families work through difficulties and form stronger, more loving relationships. Their research led to an understanding of anger as often a mask or cover for deeper emotions. This can be any range or combination of emotions, including grief, jealousy, loneliness, fear, anxiety, exhaustion, pain, embarrassment – the list goes on. Normally when activating the lesson we only get to see the tip of the iceberg until the learner starts to present a range of different emotions and behaviours which sometimes indicate there are things happening beneath the surface. We know learners operate best when their physical, mental and social needs are met. I can remember several times in my teaching career learners coming to class hungry, tired due to lack of sleep or personal things happening outside of school. Getting them to do any work at the start of the lesson was difficult. I usually thought their resistance or lack of engagement was due to something I had done or their ability to access the classwork. The things I found useful were not to respond negatively, argue or take things personally, to seek support and help from other colleagues and avoid trying to deal with things on my own. My advice is that when starting the class activity we need to actively listen to learners' remarks as they begin the activity; sometimes these are major cues into how they feel.

Short rhyme: Some learners may grumble, even appear to crumble, start the activity then stumble or get the instructions jumbled.

Being the vigilant teacher who captures the social interaction at the start of the task will give you better clarity when supporting learners. Over my practice I have learned to 'listen' to the grumbles and respond in ways that are supportive rather than clash verbally.

PERSONAL EXPERIENCE

In my early days of teaching once I had finished explaining the lesson objectives and then allowed learners to commence the main activity I would normally try to micromanage the situation. This meant I would go back to explaining the lesson objectives or spoon feeding the learners through the activity. I had a very loud and commanding voice and this caused everyone in the room to pay attention and listen. My failure was not to consider how much the level of sound in the learning space had an impact on triggering the noise levels and the class morale: learners would try to talk over my voice to have conversations with their peers. This meant that my voice was lost for some in this growing cacophony. No doubt this led to frustration and impatience on my part because the learners would not approach the work as expected. On reflection I believe it was my anxiety getting the better of me, and the fear of not getting the start of the lesson checklist right that led me to over-think the situation. To overcome this area in my teaching practice I had to learn to let go and give more ownership to learners to start the activity without me micromanaging. Also, I had to get the attention of the listeners before delivering important messages. This meant I had to up my performance, to be more thoughtful when I planned my lessons, and ensure the support materials provided enough guidance at the start of the activity. My overall aim was to help the learners take steps towards monitoring their work independently at this stage in the lesson. Why? Because if the lesson has a particular route and the start is correct, then the learners are more likely to get to the learning destination and achieve the learning outcomes. The new approach to my teaching, giving my learners more space and reducing the tendency to micromanage, inspired my learners and made the class much more focused on the lesson objectives. Strange that. By doing less at this stage in the lesson, my learners achieved more. This gave me more time to support individual learners, and support learners of different abilities. Also, I was able to be more mobile than being stationed at the front of the class. Overall I was able to decentralise the learning experience by getting learners to use the learning materials, and allow the class to root out any misconceptions before they relied on me.

 HINTS & TIPS

- **Record the lesson objectives (audio or visually)**
- **Record the lesson activities (audio or visually)**
- **Create a digital checklist using the VLEs Word or spreadsheet application then share with learners**
- **Get learners into a routine – Before I ask the teacher have I checked the learning materials and asked a peer?**

ANOTHER TEACHER'S EXPERIENCE: CARDELLA BRYCE (PRIMARY SCHOOL TEACHER)

When I reflect on the classes I have been responsible for in my career as a primary school teacher since 2012, I notice that there appear to be two common trends that I found with the cohort of pupils coming through the school: these are challenges with behaviour and learning difficulties. I know this because, being regarded by the managers as one of the stronger teachers, I have been given doubly challenging groups; and I've welcomed this challenge. The abilities in these classes have ranged from children unable to write numbers beyond 11 or spell simple CVC words (e.g. c-a-t) without assistance to the children that are working at Year 6 level in my Year 3 class. Let me be honest, I am often astonished at how pupils can reach the age of eight and not have the fundamental foundation for them to build on. When teaching, I have to ask myself:

- Have all children had the same experiences in order to access the learning?
- How will I provide that experience so they can access the learning?
- What are the steps to create the foundation, and how can I build on that foundation?

For a child to access the learning and activate their minds, they need to be equipped with the correct resources. Good resources help to facilitate learning and in turn increase independence. This is why understanding their prior experiences, interactions and base knowledge is essential to assisting with scaffolding. These resources could take the form of pictures as a visual guide, a word mat for spelling and recognising names of objects, use of dienes/base 10s in a maths session for place value and multiple digit numbers. I encourage exploration and making mistakes.

Openly, I let learners know that the greatest learning comes from making errors and there is no harm in getting something wrong en route to grasping an idea. This leads to a reduction of fear of failure and promotes risk taking. It is important to build the child's confidence for their learning so they never feel incapable. Confidence here reduces disruptions and increases their self-motivation, which is usually shown by their desire to tackle tasks independently. I help to boost their confidence through repetition and interventions. I can be quite theatrical in the classroom.

One special tool of mine is using music and songs. It is the easiest way to help a child remember anything. Think about how we learnt the alphabet, our nursery rhymes or the lyrics of the songs playing on the radio. My mother taught my brother and me how to spell our names through song! Repetition enables faster learning outcomes. In class, I make rhymes, raps, songs and dance moves to get the children active. Not only does it help those who are slightly behind, but it also benefits all learners with a catchy way to trigger their memory during assessments.

This is how I taught an underachieving learner their times tables, vowels and remembering the word class for features like nouns, verbs and adjectives. Repeat songs in the week and it will be planted in the child's mind. Try it and see.

It's all about having fun! What are the gaps? What does the child need to access the learning or work towards accessing the learning? What are the steps required? Is this gap relevant to one child or more than one? Is this something that the teaching assistant can do (if shown and modelled the steps) or does it require my own expertise? These are the questions I ask myself when devising my intervention groups.

These are used to supply children with the stepping stones to bridge the gap to understanding. Pre-teaching can give the child an insight into what will be taught, and introduce vocabulary required for the session. Establishing the gaps, how much is already known, and beginning to build from the basics upwards, develops their confidence and encourages the drive for achieving goals, especially when they themselves can see the progress.

So how might I activate a challenge? In a nutshell I use progression stages to build confidence and encourage the learners to go on and accept and try the challenge before them. I present an easy task that the child can easily complete (e.g. 10 × 3), followed by a task that requires them to apply their learning (e.g. 10 × 33) and finish with a challenge which requires additional working out (e.g. 100 × 33). The challenge should require the application of the taught skill but one step above the previous step. Even if the child gets it incorrect, praise is given for perseverance. Explain, model, and try again. Soon learning challenges will not be a thing to fear.

Also, I am mindful of my high attainers. They need to be challenged and pushed to their maximum. Higher attainers can be assigned as mentors to help consolidate their own learning through explaining to others or have an extension to further develop their understanding. To check a learner's understanding, I would pose a practice question(s) to the class and have them discuss in pairs and share answers. Or I leave a mark (mark as they complete their learning) and check for misconceptions.

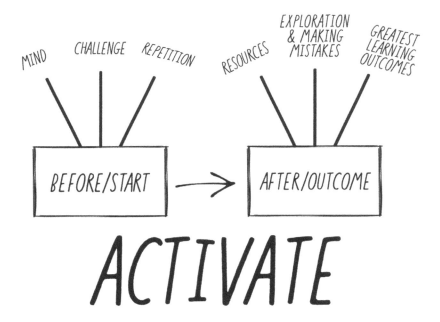

SOCIAL MEDIA

Join the conversation by using the hashtag #myteachingroutine on social media. Share with other educators how you activate your lesson. You can showcase your example through a photo, video, presentation slide or post.

CHAPTER 4
[FACILITATE]

 Teaching is not about just setting work and sitting back. It's your questioning strategies, pacing and monitoring of progress that make the big difference. - Mark Martin

OVERVIEW

THIS CHAPTER EXPLORES THE FOLLOWING IDEAS:

* THERE ARE CLEAR DIFFERENCES BETWEEN TEACHING AND FACILITATING
* QUICK AND TIMELY FEEDBACK KEEPS THE LEARNER ON TRACK
* CONSTANT, EFFECTIVE QUESTIONING SHOULD BE USED TO CHALLENGE KNOWLEDGE AND MISCONCEPTIONS
* POSITIVE PRAISE AND ENCOURAGEMENT CAN MOVE MOUNTAINS AND PROMOTE HEALTHY ACHIEVEMENT

This chapter explores the power of facilitating learning, guiding learners from the side instead of being centre stage. Traditionally the teacher is seen as the fountain of knowledge at the front of the class, pouring out information to learners. Let's explore this further. The teacher being 'the fountain of knowledge' is where learners expect that the teacher will provide knowledge and insight on the subject matter. As a result, the learners become over-reliant on the teacher to provide answers or reveal the learning destination point before they have started the learning journey. This can lead learners not to consider the content of the lesson critically or cross-reference what has been delivered by the teacher, whether it is delivered verbally, in a display like a PowerPoint presentation, or from the pages of a textbook. The side effect of this style of teaching is that learners are over-reliant on their teachers to quickly give them the microwave answers as soon as they get stuck.

FACILITATING LEARNING

Facilitated learning is where the teacher does less teaching so that the learner can do more discovering. This style allows the teacher to create a space where learners use their class book, learning materials and prior knowledge to guide their learning. The teacher may signpost different locations but doesn't easily lead the learner to the destination. Through this method learners become proactive in self-development and honing their independent skills.

However, for this approach to work teachers need to see themselves as the facilitator rather than the traditional teacher standing at the front of the class. They need to guide the learning from a coaching perspective which is mobile, quick and straight to the point. An example of a teacher being a facilitator would be a PE lesson, where they are circling around the sports hall looking at learners' technique in striking a tennis racket. They are either demonstrating the correct technique or providing concise advice. They avoid providing lengthy feedback but give enough information for the learner to keep on practising. They don't take the racket and start playing because that will limit the time with the rest of the class. Also they don't spend extra time talking to one specific learner. They might pause the whole session to reset the class, get another learner to help their peers or get the learner to watch a video clip of the technique. The teacher is mobile, providing quick and snappy advice to move learners on.

The ingredients for good facilitation involve building trust and support and creating an open dialogue with learners. Irrespective of the positive or negative feedback you may get back from your learners, use it to build greater pathways for moving the learning forward. The most important part of facilitating learning is keeping the learner focused on what they need to do independently and knowing what to do when they are stuck. Learners can easily drift off task in this type of teaching style, but that may not be a bad thing if the teacher broadens the dialogue to speak on personal development, soft skills and future employment.

FACILITATING THE ENVIRONMENT

The classroom environment normally includes good lighting, ventilation and acoustics. I repeat, normally, and I am aware that this is not the case for all teachers. In recent years interactive smart boards, wi-fi and portable devices have enabled teaching to become more engaging and mobile. The inclusion of the smart board can be used as a platform for limitless activities, ranging from interactive demonstrations, showing learners' work to the class, to using sound and animations to support the learning content and the ability to interact with the presentation through touch. In at least one sense the use of digital technology has removed the focus from the teacher being the fountain of knowledge to learners accessing information from various sources. This comes with its own challenges of teaching learners to read sources critically and to check the validity and reliability of sources. Many learners click on the first link on the web, which is most of the time a definition from Wikipedia or an internet ad. This potentially causes the issue of learners using either inappropriate or incorrect information. I normally advise learners to check three sources before they use information from the internet. However, aligning pedagogy to learning spaces is a great way to implement learner-centred learning which focuses on enabling them to learn in a decentralised fashion. Decentralising the classroom fosters a discovery zone where learners use their environment to explore knowledge through their peers, teacher, technology or surroundings; but this needs to be encouraged actively. Decentralising the classroom enables the teacher to use the environment to create spaces for learners to progress with their learning independently as well as collaboratively. Teachers can support the learner by giving one-to-one feedback or setting up mini feedback groups. The main goal is for the learner to make progress in their learning. Another approach is getting learners to present their work to the whole class from a non-central place as the learners would know that they would not necessarily need to be at the front of the learning space to present to the group, and this can help to motivate their peers to present too. By personalising the environment the teacher has a greater awareness and view of the learners' needs. The challenge for the teachers will be to keep track of progress and retain control of the entire classroom space despite learners doing different things as the lesson proceeds; this would be a positive challenge.

EVOLVING LEARNING SPACES

There has been research published on learning spaces and whether redesigning the classroom would inspire greater facilitation and more learning. The studies indicate that a combination of blended learning and reimagined physical learning spaces can lead to better learner engagement and achievement. What I have found interesting is considering this concept of learning spaces in the wake of the Covid-19 pandemic. With closed schools and attempted roll out of online teaching and learning, at times the vast majority of learners had to work remotely or were expected to engage in a blended environment, which was a drastic shift in the way learners were taught traditionally. Instead of standing in front of a classroom, we teachers were sitting in front of a camera delivering lessons, and for some teachers, there was no formal training to teach or deliver lessons in this way. So what did this mean? It meant we couldn't spend all of our time talking or giving instructions. We were forced to be more creative, from using breakout rooms to employing polls to keep learners engaged. We had to reimagine the physical and non-physical space to encourage learners to engage and participate; and let us not forget that some learners took the option not to turn on their cameras, which meant we couldn't tell if they were engaged or participating in the online lessons, or not. The pandemic has shown us, irrespective of the circumstance and the setting, building effective relationships between the teacher and the learners is paramount. For me that's the foundation of great teaching and learning.

FACILITATING QUESTIONING

As you begin to facilitate learning in the classroom, questioning is a highly effective way to check understanding, challenge learners' thinking, or even to root out misconceptions. The types of questions that could be used in the learning space include closed, open, probing, and the style of questioning can build from closed, open, and probing. Questioning maintains the flow of learning within the classroom and allows the learner to participate within the lesson. There are various ways questioning can take place in the classroom from verbal, sticky notes, writing feedback in books or sending a message online. To make the process manageable you might have some pre-written questions which are levelled and they could be handed out to learners as you circle the class. The learner's response will inform you whether they are on track with the work or they need further assistance. To avoid learners clashing you might want to have some rules on constructive feedback and responding appropriately, as mentioned in Chapter 1 on connecting. Some teachers may get learners to create their own set of questions for their peers or revision materials. Let me add, it is important for the teacher to read signs of prosodic features in the question and answer exchanges as well as the body language of the learners; and a keen, honest and ever-increasing knowledge of diversity and unpatronising patience on the teacher's part are crucial here.

 HINTS & TIPS

1. **Put a time limit on the amount of time you spend with each learner**
2. **Feedforward from written steps to constructive advice**
3. **Provide feedback without giving the learner the answer straight away**
4. **Get learners to explain what they have learned to their peers**

MULTIPLE ROLES

The questioning strategies, pacing and monitoring of progress makes a big difference when getting learners to reach their academic goals. How does a teacher support their learners simultaneously, with their different needs and abilities? To solve this major challenge teachers spend a considerable amount of time planning schemes of work that are differentiated and matched to their learners' abilities. In order for teachers to navigate the classroom they have multiple roles, which, among others, include classroom manager, facilitator and instructor.

Manager: As a manager they control the classroom climate and atmosphere by setting out the standards, expectations, materials and furniture of the room. Learners acknowledge they have to operate within the manager's framework, but are given the freedom to commence the work at their own pace.

Facilitator: As a facilitator they monitor the learners' performance during an activity. They are on standby to provide feedback, advice and guidance to learners. The facilitator uses other learners and additional resources around them, so they are not dealing with one individual for a specific amount of time.

Instructor: As an instructor they demonstrate what the learner should be doing and ensure that they are following the specific instructions given. They review the learners' performance and provide actionable advice and feedback on their ability. This role is normally useful when you have small groups or are working with specific learners.

MANAGER

Lifeguard

FACILITATOR

Music Instructor

INSTRUCTOR

Sports Coach

Every school and classroom is different, and operates in different ways. When teachers are facilitating learning they need to be adaptable to new ways of working and allowing learners to lead their own learning. As already mentioned, the key to great facilitation is not surfing around a classroom trying to engage with them individually, but making sure every interaction with learners is purposeful for their academic and personal development. There will be times when learners may not want to engage or distract their peers in this type of model. In these situations you want to reset the room or seek support from another colleague for learners not willing to engage.

LEARNER-LED

Facilitating learning is not a straightforward process; as a teacher you have to role model what you want your learners to be, then give them the space and opportunity to grow through your approach and examples. When getting learners to explain what they have learned, they can then demonstrate to their peers. That's where the magic happens, because learners are no longer passive but active in showcasing to others their learning journey. The benefits are endless, from developing their soft skills to contributing positively to their class environment. You may start off with small tasks which encourage learners to take some role in contributing to the lesson. Over time, as learners grow in confidence, you want to increase their participation and give them far more active roles in group or class presentations. Getting learners to see the value of ownership of their work is priceless because they take more responsibility for completing work and supporting others. Learner-led lessons build confidence between the learner and teacher which helps to develop trust and to learners taking risks, knowing their teacher is the safety net. To cultivate this level of connection takes time and patience because some learners are shy and afraid of being condemned by their peers. As a result some learners may avoid presenting or participating in group discussion. That's perfectly fine, it shouldn't be forced or an uncomfortable experience. You may want to provide prompts or scripts for learners if they need extra support. I usually remind my learners that whether they like it or not they need to lead on things in the outside world, and the classroom is the supportive training ground to lead, inspire, and even make mistakes. 'Have a go,' I encourage, 'and see how it feels to present your ideas to people in the room!'

HINTS & TIPS

Here are some powerful questions to ask your learners as you facilitate their learning:

1.   **What do you think …?**
2.   **Why do you think that …?**
3.   **How do you know this …?**
4.   **Can you tell me more about it?**
5.   **What if …?**

Task: Create some questions about your subject matter.

POSITIVE GUIDANCE

Being a teacher you are tasked to teach and deliver engaging content to your learners, but being a facilitator you are tasked to guide your learners through the learning process. The facilitator role is to remove themselves from the centre stage of the class and empower learners individually to take their own centre stage in their learning. Reorganising the classroom where the learner is not dependent on the teacher at the front of the room takes some time to normalise. Supporting learners through the lesson activity, the facilitator needs to encourage the learner to try to complete the lesson activities with minimal assistance. Helping learners become independent in their learning helps build confidence and resilience. The relationship between the teacher and learner alters; it becomes similar to a personal trainer helping someone to work on their physique. This means you as the teacher need to be conscious of your interaction with your learners; for example, being conscious of your body language, language, tone, timing and presence. Being an effective facilitator requires you to raise the morale, self-esteem and confidence in learners as they progress through the task(s) or the lesson content. The teacher's role is to be the guide on the side, encouraging their learners to reach new heights. Learners need to feel and believe that the teacher is invested in their achievements irrespectively of how big or small they may be. The challenge with positive guidance is getting the balance right. If learners hear the same words over and over again, then the words soon lose their value and impact. However, when you are genuine and sincere in your approach for the majority of the time the learners can see that you have their best interests at heart. As a facilitator, be mindful of how much time you spend with each learner because it may create tension amongst learners or give them the impression you have favourites. This means you have to balance your time with each learner and interaction has to be concise. Another method of positive guidance is to utilise the reward system, which shows/honours the class's or individuals' performance in lessons.

FEEDFORWARD

Feedforward is a development approach to giving learners feedback in completing a task. While feedback focuses on a learner's current ability, feedforward looks ahead and offers constructive guidance on how to do better. Learners normally receive feedback in formative and summative formats which aid their learning and indicate whether they are making progress. The feedforward approach works two to three steps ahead from where the learning is currently performing. Each advanced step should be accessible and relatable to the learner's learning journey. The feedforward can take many forms, from written steps to constructive advice. This approach helps to deliver high quality dialogue around learning, and clarifies what good learning should look like in terms of goals, criteria or standards set. Another area of feedforward is developing a growth mindset where the learner is challenged to think about the next phase of their learning and trigger a deeper analysis of how they are currently performing. The main aim is to build confidence and self-esteem – to keep on going despite the challenges and difficulty the work may present.

CLASS EXAMPLE

In my Year 10 computer science class, my learners were quick to look at the grade and not the feedback written in their end of term exams. So I had to come up with some creative ways to encourage learners to read the feedback and act on it. This is when I decided to use feedforward, which takes their current grade and shows the key items they need to complete. Here is an example of the normal feedback we provide to learners at the end of each term:

> Well done Student A you have explained the difference between RAM and ROM which is a level 3 but in order to achieve a grade 4 you have to state the limitations and benefits. If you can add 3–4 lines with some technical terms for both items you will be on target to getting a good end of year grade.

The challenge I had was to convert the traditional feedback into tangible steps that the learners could interpret and move their learning forward. Some learners didn't know how to construct the three or four lines with technical terms. This meant I had to write some examples of what a good response looks like and what technical terms could be used. Surprisingly, learners paid serious attention to the feedback.

I sent them the feedback via the school's VLE. I then circled the room to ensure they were acting on the feedback. Similar to in the PE lesson, the teacher needs to be mobile, relatable and relevant. There is no specific formula for feedforward, but it involves a combination of praise, real time feedback and giving some advice on what the learners need to do in the future. The thing that gels it all together is the learner being accountable for their next step or action.

SYNCHRONOUS VS ASYNCHRONOUS LEARNING

Synchronous learning is done in real time with learners and teachers in the same location. Asynchronous learning is where content (e.g. videos and presentations) can be accessed 24/7 in any location. There are both limitations and benefits with facilitating online learning because there are many factors (i.e. equipment, connectivity and attitudes) beyond the teacher's control that may hinder the learning experience. Live teaching is a great way to have real time dialogue with your learners but unless you have different activities to do, it can be a very passive experience if the teacher is doing most of the talking. Recording lessons and uploading them for learners to access in their own time is great, but you might need to have some materials that quiz learners on the content. The common themes with online learning are that it has to be engaging, materials have to be accessible and the learner can see progress.

During the pandemic, I was delivering a graphic design module where learners had to create a poster about an issue that affects them in their local area. The work was set on the VLE and learners had a week to work on their poster. The first online lesson was to teach the learners about the different things they can do with the graphic design tools. Learners engaged in the session by asking questions and practising some of the skills. A week later learners came back with different designs and took turns to showcase their progress and receive feedback. When providing learners feedback, I allowed them to share their screen and present their work. The learners had to take notes on the feedback given by myself and their peers. One learner went a step further and demonstrated some skills that they learned beyond the assignment. It was great to see learners taking the initiative and innovating in their own time. The following week we reviewed this learner's work and to my surprise they had followed the feedback and produced a professional poster on the topic of knife crime.

As this was a creative module, facilitating this type of lesson was fun and straightforward. However, learners struggled to process some of the complex topics and instructions for independent learning when I taught live online for an exam-based module. The quality of work was not good to begin with but after changing the format by breaking the complex topics into bite size chunks and making sure the work I set for independent learning matched the learners' ability I saw a better response from the learners. Also, putting learners into virtual groups helped to reduce the class size and give opportunity for quieter learners to engage. Motivating themselves to do work independently was the key to getting them to attempt the work.

Teachers who struggle with technology need to upskill or get left behind. It is as clear and as simple as that! It's unfortunate, but that's the terrain for teaching in schools and online now. You can upskill by attending Continuous Professional Development (CPD) sessions, shadowing other teachers, or trying activities that cultivate online learning. Implementing new tech and innovation takes time, and continual practice is required.

PERSONAL EXPERIENCE

My initial teacher training prepared me for classroom management, teaching pedagogies and different ways to deliver content. It didn't prepare me for a world of online teaching or using education technologies in new and innovative ways. I had learned a lot of these skills through attending external CPD events, online training and teacher networks. After going on countless training sessions I started to develop new ways, using edtech tools, to inspire learners within my classroom. From using classroom monitoring tools to creating video tutorials for learners to access key points of the lessons, I realised that I could make learning more fun, simplify my workload, and showcase good examples to teachers around the world. I understood that tech is another tool that we can use to encourage learners to become independent. So instead of doing whole class lectures I was able to signpost learners to my presentations, video recordings and practice exam questions. This meant I was more mobile around the classroom because I didn't need to gain everyone's attention to guide the learning. I was able to personalise the learning and allow learners to work at their own pace. The new approach propelled me into becoming a facilitator where I would approach learners individually to see if they were on track, ask personalised questions to check misconceptions, and give quiet words of encouragement. The behaviour in my class improved because there was no room for learners to distract each other; if they were all working at different stages. Some of the learners that excelled under this approach were appointed as mini helpers and they would assist me with facilitating the session. They would be the ones to support their peers or come to the front of the class and explain their findings.

Let's be real – facilitating a lesson can become a very consuming process because you are always on the move and trying to support learners at their different learning stages. To keep control of the process I would normally have the levels or lesson outcomes on the board as I circled the room. This meant my teacher talk was short, concise and focused. Now trying to blend this experience to online learning was a challenge. I taught my learners to access the course content online and when they got stuck to post their questions on our internal forum on the VLE. The live lessons were difficult because the majority of learners had their cameras off, which meant you couldn't see their faces or emotions. Also you couldn't see if they were taking notes and paying attention as I covered the different parts of the scheme of work. I would frequently stop and start the online session and ask a series of questions to ensure learners were listening and focused on the content. The style of questions were structured and learners had the opportunity to respond verbally or through the chat function. Also, I got learners to think of their own questions to ask me during the session, which gave them another reason to pay close attention.

There are a lot of unknowns when facilitating online learning but you need to keep a cool head and have a backup resource if the internet connection goes down or technology fails. However, online learning particularly worked for learners that had the confidence, the technological environment and support at home; but for the learners that didn't have this structure, engagement and lesson participation were minimal. When the lockdown eased we still kept the hybrid model of teaching online and offline. When I saw the learners that didn't engage online face to face, I noticed that the human connection had re-energised them to engage with course and content. There is no silver bullet to facilitating a lesson online and offline. The aim is to remove all the barriers that might hinder their learning and develop a bond where learners feel comfortable to attempt tasks on their own. Teachers need to continually develop themselves and understand the different types of technologies that can be used to facilitate learning and drive engagement and participation.

HINTS & TIPS

1. Create a glossary/FAQ to support learners when they are stuck
2. Try feedforward, which can take many forms, from written steps to constructive advice
3. Monitor your tone, voice and style when providing feedback to learners
4. Be mindful of the time you take when providing feedback to each learner

ANOTHER TEACHER'S EXPERIENCE: OSI EJIOFOR (ASSISTANT HEADTEACHER – PRIMARY SCHOOL)

I am a strong advocate of the teacher becoming the facilitator rather than only being the instructor. I was inspired by a TED talk given by Professor Sugata Mitra in 2013; he shared results from his experiment using a hole in the wall computer in the slums of Kalkaji, Delhi in 1999, then throughout rural India and again in Cambodia in 2004. He found that students were able to learn by experimentation and exploration. He called this approach Minimally Invasive Education. In some cases students were able to teach themselves how to use computers by themselves without the instruction of a teacher. At the turn of the millennium that was an important discovery, but now we see this occur in very young children who get hold of the technology in their household. Toddlers are able to use iPads and other devices to access activities and watch things they like, without adult instruction or supervision. The findings of Professor Mitra's experiment as well as the experiences I had at home with my own children and their use of technology, reignited the flames that were burning inside me regarding the hindrance to learning that often takes place in the classroom.

It seemed to me that there was a natural desire and curiosity to learn within all of us, and it seems that such curiosity is stifled once students leave the Early Years Foundation Stage (EYFS). In EYFS students are able to explore their environment and learn through pre-planned activities and spaces that encourage and facilitate learning without the need for deep instructional intervention from a teaching practitioner. Once in Year 1, students abandon this model and slot into the instructional, often passive, learning model, which then continues throughout their school life. These studies also led me to research constructivism and learn how a constructivist approach to teaching may be more beneficial to the learner as it can continue this EYFS style of approach to facilitating learning. Cognitive constructivism facilitates students using their prior knowledge to build on what they know and increase their knowledge from that standpoint, while social constructivism enables students to learn through interacting and sharing with one another. All of these findings have helped me to become more of a facilitator in the classroom when teaching, thus allowing students to learn through curiosity, collaboration, creative and critical thinking and being stuck.

When applying these approaches I have not experienced a lesson in which 'it hasn't worked' (learning has not taken place) or has markedly gone wrong. I have, however, seen students progress in ways that have really surprised me. For example, I was teaching a Year 3 class and decided to set a 'big question' (based on what I learned from Sugata Mitra's classroom in the cloud) rather than a standard learning objective. The lesson was about time, and teaching time is one of the most difficult lessons to teach a Year 3 child. The concepts of seconds not being second but possibly first, the idea of to and past, quarters and halves, the intervals and subintervals can all be quite difficult concepts for children to understand when teaching instructionally. Therefore I wanted to have a lesson that served as both formative assessment as well as facilitating a significant learning journey for the students. The question was: What is time and how is it measured? I gave the class iPads, enough for one between two, and asked them to use Apple Keynote to collect and present their answers to my question. The only problem for the class was that they had never used Keynote before and they were not allowed to ask me how to use it (the natural reflex for a Year 3 child who has had a mostly instructional approach to education). They were allowed to help the pair that was close to them but they were not allowed to focus on formatting their information until they had collected it all. They were to begin with what they knew and then add to their knowledge using the internet. They were initially given 15 minutes to complete the task. This was to add a sense of urgency and ensure they were focused. I always had in mind to give them 40 minutes so I rewarded them with an extra 15 minutes because they were working so well, and then rewarded another 5 minutes to help them complete their slides. They were very grateful for my generosity.

THE ART OF MODELLING

Students   Teacher

Once completed, the students were given time to present their findings to the class by mirroring their tablet to the board in presentation mode (also something they had never done before). I was amazed at what was shared. The students were in mixed ability pairs and were asked to divide their presentation between them. They shared information on sundials, analogue and digital, post and antemeridian, Peter Henlien, Archimedes, hourglass, egg timers, facts about the clock tower and Big Ben and so much more. The class was asked to take notes on a whiteboard while others presented in order to be able to ask questions about their presentation. This facilitated students learning from each pair and adding to the knowledge they had as well as reinforcing the understanding of the presenters. I taught a lesson without giving much instruction at all. I didn't teach the students how to use Keynote at all, they helped each other. By taking away the linear approach to learning the students were able to learn more. The students were fully engaged throughout the lesson and the class did not want the lesson to end.

My advice to new or returning teachers would be to do your best to encourage, or model a facilitative approach to teaching in order to improve learning and then share your experiences with your colleagues. It is better to show what has already worked rather than to encourage others to do what you haven't already proven. I would also advise that they read up on some of the studies and findings of people such as Sugata Mitra, Lev Vygotsky, Phillip Scott, Jean Piaget, John Dewey and others who have explored a constructivist approach to facilitating learning.

SOCIAL MEDIA

Join the conversation by using the hashtag #myteachingroutine on social media. Share with other educators how you facilitate learning in your classroom. You can showcase your example through a photo, video, presentation slide or post.

CHAPTER 5
[COLLABORATE]

 Working together gives us the ability to see the world in new ways. - Mark Martin

OVERVIEW

THIS CHAPTER EXPLORES THE FOLLOWING IDEAS:

* COLLABORATION REQUIRES DETAILED PLANNING
* COLLABORATION IS BASED ON RELATIONSHIPS, CONFLICTS AND PROBLEM SOLVING
* COLLABORATION DECENTRALISES THE LEARNING
* TECHNOLOGY WILL ENABLE LEARNERS TO CONTRIBUTE IN NEW AND EXCITING WAYS

The aim of this stage of the *My Teaching Routine* model is to show learners how to collaborate and provide learning experiences which enable them to collaborate. In a sense it is cyclical. Collaboration in lessons helps to get learners to share, lead and encourage their peers and simultaneously benefit from the exercise. Collaborative learning includes problem solving, dealing with conflict, being inclusive and being organised. There will be a range of encounters that our learners will face once they've left the world of school and schooling, so collaborating in school settings should prove to be valuable preparation for the real world and nurture enduring life skills. Platforms for collaborative learning offer the teacher the opportunity to build leadership skills for all learners, promote ownership, and create a better classroom environment for all who engage.

THE CHALLENGE

It must be stated that real collaboration is difficult to achieve and does not happen by itself. If we want organic collaboration amongst learners, we need to intentionally design it as part of our teaching routine, and again, putting in the extra effort will reap rewards. I believe that learners should learn how to collaborate and be shown what good collaborations could produce in a conducive setting. You may want to start by allocating leadership roles and tasks and giving examples to the class. Then create subgroups for learners to tackle the problem or respond to the challenge. There are always teething problems with groups around personalities, friends and even skivers, so you need to be alert to potential conflicts or groups falling apart due to lack of engagement.

COLLABORATIVE LEARNING

Over the last decades, research has demonstrated that collaborative learning can promote academic and social educational outcomes (Johnson et al., 2007). Many of today's job roles involve people working together within departments, groups, teams and many other settings. For example, in the U.S. the military uses a powerful exercise called After-Action Review (AAR) (U.S. Army Board Study Guide, 2006), which allows teams to learn from their own experiences. AAR consists of four direct questions:

1.   What did we intend to do?
2.   What were our actual results?
3.   What explains our results? What do we want to sustain?
4.   What do we want to change moving forward?

These questions can definitely be used in our classrooms when getting learners to work together. Effective collaboration is when everyone is clear on what they need to do and what is the desired outcome. Collaborative learning allows each individual to analyse material, synthesise what they know and feed that back into the group's objectives. The aim is for learners to realise the benefits of working in a group and the power of working with others. If they appreciate working in a group involves looking after each other and working through differences, it helps to make the experience more impactful. To help learners begin working together, you may start with low stakes activities that will encourage them to get involved in a group activity.

An example of a low stakes activity is getting the group to investigate an environmental problem in their local area and then allowing them to present and get feedback on their findings to the group. Then you can point out to the learners that all knowledge is socially constructed and without the sharing of ideas and perspectives no learning takes place. Helping learners to explore new ways of thinking with their peers helps to build their own understanding.

After getting learners comfortable working with their peers you might want to allocate learners into different teams in which their skill sets and attitudes will be able to thrive. This may be a daunting task because you are having to dismantle your classroom and put it back together. During this stage the noise level may rise, learners may protest, and you may be asked several questions like, 'Why do we have to do this?' In other words, you will be challenged as you take the learners beyond their comfort zones. I have found that one way of combating any resistance that arises is being organised with team names on something topical (i.e. Company A). When I have assigned a leader to the group they read out the instructions to their peers, which keeps their peers in check and usually fosters peer engagement. Each person in the group is allocated a specific task or activity they will need to complete. To sustain a rich collaborative experience with a competitive edge and focus you might want to add a leader board to reward positive soft skills for the completion of the group task. The aim is to get learners to be supportive of each other and share ideas to enhance their learning. This exercise calls for good, clear communication where the learners could draw from a bank of words and the words in this bank could/should be organised for different stages of the collaborative activity. Ahead of the lesson I have given attention to the physical space and the layout of the classroom. The classroom can appear to be a barrier if the tables and chairs cannot be moved to create a collaborative environment. This is where the teacher might need to be creative when getting learners to work together.

PEER LEARNING COMMUNITIES

Peer learning is not a new idea, and featured in educational discussions in the 1960s in global education discourse. Different education thought leaders like Vygotsky (1962), Piaget (1971) and Bandura (1977) have argued that social learning is better than learning alone. Social learning is the idea that learners learn from observing others. This can be broken down into three areas:

Attention: Learners can't learn if they are distracted or are not focused on the task. In order for learners' attention to be focused on the learning, teachers need to ensure learners are engaged, active and involved in the learning experience. The social element is learners regulating each other to stay on task without losing focus.

Retention: Storing information into long-term memory is a challenging process for learners. Many learners will use revision techniques such as flash cards to memorise information. In a social learning context learners utilise their peers to test, probe and talk about the topics they have learned. This helps learners to recall that information and use it where necessary.

Reproduction: Learners support each other by unpacking, packing and repacking their learning together. The bonding between learners may help to build confidence through shared experiences and develop interpersonal skills. The points above tend to work if learners are determined to work together, and let's be real, this determination to work together is not always a feature when all learners interact.

Effective peer learning communities can be hindered if the relationships, togetherness and communication among the learners are in conflict, or simply if the communication breaks down. This means, just like a theatre production, the teacher might need to put on rehearsals or stage the performance so the community is built modelling good standards and routines.

Peer learning communities remind me of the online community Reddit, where people post questions and answers on different topics within the group. The community has rules that members need to follow in order not to be removed from the group. Some groups have moderators that help to support the questions being asked and the upkeep of the community.

The community is sustained by individual queries, interest and fruitful conversations. Adopting the Reddit framework into the classroom requires quite a few stakeholders that can support the teacher and the ecosystem. It could work if the teacher could train A-Level learners to be group moderators and contributors. These learners then support GCSE learners when they post a question or discussion item. The older learners may be given time in their after-school programme or during tutorial time to support younger learners.

Everyone in the ecosystem benefits and develops professional skills way beyond the scope of the course and institution. I tried this Reddit framework with my GCSE (14–16 years) learners and first year university (18+) learners. I fostered the partnership through a close connection with the local university. The university learners were assigned to help my GCSE learners develop a mobile phone application to support refugees. We had gone through the activity with all participants before they met in person.

The GCSE learners commenced with the activity and the university learners supported their progress by giving advice where needed. When the GCSE learners created a prototype, the university learners were able to give feedback remotely. The impact this had made on the GCSE prototype was amazing, and the university participants grew in confidence in providing effective support. During the showcase event where the GCSE learners had to present their work the university learners attended the event for moral support. Overall, the whole process was fantastic and very rewarding for everyone involved.

So then, what are the advantages of peer learning communities? Peer learning communities here are seen to make learning accessible in and out of the classroom. They help learners to move away from being solely dependent on the teacher and take steps to use each other as sources of knowledge, and the learners are inspired to take further steps towards independent collaborative learning.

CLASSROOM EXPERIENCE

Once I did a risk lesson (an experiential lesson that schools allow you to have during an academic year) where I placed Year 10 computer science learners into groups to work on a problem statement around cyber security. They had to design a presentation for primary school learners on the dangers of using the internet and how they could safeguard themselves. The class was mixed ability and some learners had issues with socialising with their peers. So I broke the activity into four parts – research, design, presentation and presentation delivery to the class. Each member of the group was assigned a specific task, which meant everyone had to be doing something. Halfway through the activity some learners started to disrupt each other and some went off task. In my mind I thought I was losing control of the situation and the lesson was becoming chaotic. I decided to stop the lesson, get everyone's attention and show them what each of the parts should look like; I then gave them a limited amount of time to ensure they were on track. The subliminal deadline to my surprise got each group focused and they started to take the activity seriously because they didn't want to be embarrassed when presenting their work. So I quickly circled the room and gave feedback to each learner with a simple word of encouragement or comment on areas where they could improve their work. When it was time for each group to present their work each member had to explain their role and how they had contributed to the activity.

REFLECTION

On reflection I learned that group work is not a straightforward process, learners are unpredictable when it comes to collaboration. However irrespective of their mindset you have the opportunity to engage with them. You have the power to go beyond the activity by showing them how different attitudes can make and break relationships and teams.

CLASSROOM EXPERIENCE

Another example of creating a peer learning community was with my Year 12 computer science class. I created an online space on the VLE to post presentation slides, course updates and tips for examinations.

One learner decided to post an error they had encountered in Python to the main page on the online platform. The quiet learner that would not engage unless prompted in class instantly responded to the learner that had posted the online problem. The learner who was stuck communicated by shouting 'Thanks!' to the helper and gave them a like online. I didn't get involved in the exchange because I wanted to give the learners a space to provide peer feedback and exercise problem solving skills.

Knowing when to intervene in a peer learning community in the role of the teacher is crucial because it's very easy for the teacher to dominate and stop learners from contributing. I think the best indication is the time it takes for a problem to be responded to. If a few days go by without a response, then I would step in and provide the necessary feedback.

How might peer learning communities work when a school is shut during a pandemic? There is a big opportunity here to introduce online community groups or online classrooms that get learners actively participating online together. However the first thing is teachers need to be trained to manage such environments and show the benefits to their classes.

ALLOCATING ROLES WITHIN THE CLASSROOM

Collaboration doesn't need to be solely group work, it could be classroom wide where individual learners are assigned different responsibilities to support their peers and classroom climate.

Specified roles in whole class learning activities offer learners the opportunity for meaningful and focused interactions between their peers. Learners who have been given a role are likely to stay on task and pay closer attention to the task at hand. Learners with a purpose and clear responsibilities are more likely to gain a sense of confidence when they interact with their peers. The role may vary from among the following:

Motivator: Motivates peers to think through their approaches and ideas. The motivator reviews their peers' work and provides feedback based on their own work and lesson objectives. The aim of the motivator is to help challenge their peers' thinking into deeper understanding. Also they are supportive, constructive and clinical in supporting their peers in the learning environment.

Questioner: Instead of the teacher providing the questions to the group, the questioner comes up with their set of questions based on their own understanding of the topic. Instead of providing their peers with the answer the questioner will probe further with questions either supplied by the teacher or their experience. The aim of the questioner is to challenge their peers' thinking and draw out new ideas for the activity.

Checker: Checks the quality of their peers' work with regard to grammar, technical words and the presentation of ideas. The checker may highlight areas of weakness and provide practical solutions to their peers. The checker may ask their peers to explain their work or get them to demonstrate their understanding. The aim of the checker is to help their peers root out any errors or misconceptions.

I regard such roles as priceless and this is compounded positively as the teacher monitors the interaction and praises the learner for their efforts. This praise is similar to immediate and focused verbal feedback. Some learners may not want to be allocated a role or may shy away from the responsibility. It shouldn't be forced or learners made to feel guilty if they don't want to participate. The aim of the approach is to create a classroom culture of collaborative learning.

During a Key Stage 3 lesson, learners were required to write a summary on the benefits and limitations of RAM and ROM. The aim of the activity was to include technical words in their presentations. One of the learners had completed the work with lightning speed. On that occasion instead of setting the particular learner an extension task, I made them the 'technical word checker'. This role was announced to the entire class and written on the board. The 'technical word checker' had to go around the room, listen in to class talk, and see if their peers were using technical terms in their presentations. The low ability learners appreciated the input from their peers because they were able to correct themselves and see where they were going wrong. Some learners tried to use the 'technical word checker' to give them the answer, which I instructed them not to do, but to give enough hints for them to progress. Overall the activity went extremely well and the learners seemed to benefit from the experience.

REFLECTION QUESTIONS

- How often do you attempt group work in lessons?
- How might you respond to and support a team that breaks down at various stages of an activity?
- How do you engage the quiet or shy learners?

PEER-TO-PEER MARKING

Peer-to-peer marking (also known as peer assessment) is when learners use assessment criteria to make judgements about each other's work. For this to be meaningful the learner-assessor has to understand the given criteria. The learner is required to mark their peers' work, thus generating feedback and some sort of measurable result. When this is up and working in a classroom, peer-to-peer marking supports learners to gain a deeper understanding of the assessment criteria, which in turn enables the learners to assess the work of others.

During a computer science lesson with Key Stage 3, learners were asked to write a creative piece on the power of the Central Processing Unit (CPU) in Microsoft Word. After the learners wrote for 10 minutes on the topic I stopped the class, got them to swap seats, and then taught them how to peer assess each other's work. They had to select the highlighter tool then follow the instructions:

- Red highlighter – To highlight an error or missing content
- Green highlighter – To provide feedback to improve their peer's work
- Blue highlighter – To provide advice on how to achieve a higher grade

You can alter or add additional colours to the marking scheme, which could provide more options to include praise and other requirements. When observing how learners interact with the peer-to-peer assessment, it seemed to me that most of the learners were engaged and took pride in marking their peers' work. They did the task with an element of empathy and togetherness. Some learners did not feel comfortable marking their peers' work, however, so I let them assess their own by using the checklist.

Overall, peer-to-peer marking does not save you time because you still have to check the learners' marking and decide whether it meets the criteria. However, you create an open dialogue with the learners to question their reasoning behind the way they have marked their peers' work. This helps to provide an in-depth insight into the assessment criteria content and topic/course content. As a result, it gives learners confidence and an indication of how they might be assessed in the exam or activity.

DESIGN THINKING

Design Thinking is becoming a popular tool and approach to use in the classroom for collaboration. It helps the learner or teacher to become human-centred problem solvers. The collaborative workflow is designed to tackle the big problems and discover new solutions. Design Thinking was popularised by Silicon Valley design company IDEO and is now used by some of the world's leading brands such as Apple, Google, Samsung and GE. Over recent years many institutions have adopted this approach to help participants or learners become more creative and innovative in their learning and approach to new things. Design Thinking has five key principles or tenets: empathise, define, ideate, prototype and test.

Where the 'how?' and the 'why?' are unknown, the process leads to the desired goal becoming known.

Learners need to work together to solve real world, ill-defined problems; and crucially, a positive mindset is required in their work efforts to create opportunities to use their abilities and skill sets to respond to the challenge. IDEO recently published a toolkit, *Design Thinking for Educators*, which provides teachers with an in-depth guide on how to use the design principles in a range of subjects (www.ideo.com/post/design-thinking-for-educators).

Design Thinking works well across all subjects and educational settings; for example it could be used in a primary school where learners have to design a specific item using cardboard boxes, or alternatively, in a secondary school where learners have to design something using newspapers or edtech tools. Design Thinking invokes experiential learning where learners are being asked to innovate rather than memorising content for an exam. Also measuring learners' progress in this way is difficult unless you are meriting learners on their soft skills and ability to think outside the box.

CLASSROOM EXPERIENCE

In my A-Level computer science class, I got my learners to design a tech solution for elderly people using the Design Thinking toolkit (mentioned above). They were all allocated a part of the toolkit. The thing that worked well was showing learners examples of each of the stages and how they should approach the task. Having a reference point gave learners valuable context and in return they were able to produce good outcomes.

To activate the task learners were given sticky notes, A5 paper and coloured pens to write down their ideas. Then learners were placed in teams, which was slightly challenging because they wanted to be with their friends. So I then allowed them to be with their peers because the activity required all members of the team to produce tangible outputs. This meant there was no place to socialise, hide or slack. I mentioned to each group they would have a limited amount of time to research, develop and present their ideas. After moving around the room several times to check on the different groups I would prompt certain team members I felt were struggling or drifting off task. I could have provided more support resources to steer the learning but allowed the groups to independently source the information themselves. Once learners had completed their presentation, they came as a team in front of the whole class. The quality of the presentations was good because they had connected what they had learned in previous lessons and the local community challenge. The Design Thinking method enabled my learners to come up with some great solutions and prototypes.

On reflection I've done several group activities where I have used different models but Design Thinking was very effective in getting my learners to think beyond the curriculum and connect their learning to everyday scenarios. However if you were going to do this with a younger audience you might need to provide more structured resources to assist learners with their problem statement.

THE JAZZ BAND ANALOGY

Thinking about collaborative learning environments reminds me of a live jazz band, in which all the members have a shared purpose, trust and innovation. The musicians all rely on each other to share chords, follow the tempo and rhythm, and flow through the musical transitions. There's even a time within their performance where the members are given the opportunity to show off their skills with a solo piece. This helps them to be acknowledged for their contributions and efforts throughout the performance. Jazz music screams humility and togetherness; in order to put on a great show their ego, pride and attitude needs to be removed in order for their peers to have the same sound. This is teamwork and even with a unified sense of purpose, the performance needs coordinating; after all, bands have bandleaders. What can we take away from jazz bands? Each learner strives to be their best and works with real intention to support each of their co-learners as a whole. The classroom is as strong as its weakest link or learners who fail to engage with the activity or collaboration task. It's going to take one step at a time to create a culture where everyone gets to lead, do a solo and shine. The teacher is the bandleader in the initial stages of getting the learners to be familiar within this zone of collaboration, and there is no reason why learner-group-leaders cannot be bandleaders in future lessons.

PERSONAL EXPERIENCE

Collaboration is now becoming a prominent feature in the workplace, in institutions and everyday life. The more we expose learners to this style of working the better prepared they are for the future of work. The pandemic illustrated how important collaboration was amongst scientists to discover a vaccine for Covid-19. It took hundreds of leading scientists to investigate the different variants in real time and work together to find a possible solution. The challenge for the education system is how we can get our learners to collaborate online and offline. It is much more than a one-off lesson activity or featured in a risk lesson; it's a skill that is needed in all aspects of our daily lives. The main ingredients for collaboration are:

- Relationships
- Productivity
- Innovation
- Leadership
- Problem solving

There are plenty of collaboration models schools and teachers can adopt to introduce collaborative learning. It needs to be embedded into the school's ecosystem, learners should be able to see opportunities for collaboration in all their subjects and throughout their time at the institution. School leaders need to upskill or reskill their staff to ensure the quality of collaborative learning is a similar experience throughout the school. The aim is to build learner's confidence to use the tools to effectively use the scaffolding and structure learned in the classroom.

During the early stages of my teaching career I would normally associate the term 'collaboration' with noise, chaos and relinquishing control of the classroom. If I am honest, collaboration was a haze of stress. Embedding collaboration or collaborative activities into my teaching routine was difficult and it was a laborious part of my lesson planning. This task required grouping the correct learners together for the activity, ensuring the environment was correct for mini breakout groups, and matching the assignment to the group's abilities for the duration of the task. These concerns became a reality when I decided to do a risk lesson. My risk lesson was based on effective group collaboration with a mixed ability group. I had planned to break the class up into teams of four and assign each member of the group a role.

When I initiated the session the learners thought it was a time to socialise and give the most active, studious person on the team the majority of the work to do. Some individuals within the group were good at delegating the workload to each learner but did not see the value in completing the activity as a team. However, learners seemed thoroughly engaged with the activity and at the end of the group task selected learners to lead presentations to showcase their group's work. One learner took control of the presentation slides, one helped hold up their prototype and the other talked about their workflow. On reflection the risk lesson didn't go to plan as expected because I wanted learners to take more ownership of the activities but they relied on me to guide the activities. If I could do the risk lesson again I would assign a leader to each group and give a specific task to each individual with a time limit.

Also you need to know the chemistry of the group because time can be wasted sorting out conflicts or disagreements. I think for new or inexperienced teachers you might need to create a group list prior to the activity and have a code of conduct which all learners need to follow.

Despite the benefits of collaborative learning it does not come easy and may require a mindset shift for everyone involved. Understanding the different mindsets and personas when it comes to collaboration will definitely help in understanding why some find the experience joyful and some a burden. As already mentioned, the more technology brings us together, the more we have to interact with people online and offline. With the recent announcement of the 'metaverse' it looks like we are heading towards a future where we not only have to learn how to collaborate in the real world, but in the virtual world too!

ANOTHER TEACHER'S EXPERIENCE: ASHLEY HALL (HEAD OF FACULTY – SIXTH FORM COLLEGE)

I teach in a sixth form college and you would think that teaching a practical subject such as sports science and getting students to collaborate would be easy, right? Wrong!

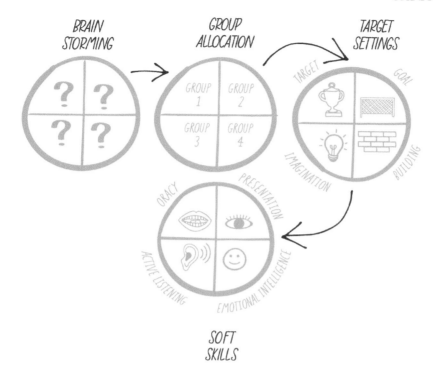

When I first started teaching, I believed that getting students to work together 'effectively' was to put them into randomly assigned groups, and, as long as the task was challenging or enjoyable, the magic of collaboration would somehow happen. 'Stretch and challenge' was on trend at the start of my career, and I thought that if I could create a way to achieve this ideal with learners at both ends of the spectrum, plus hope for some type of collaboration in group activities, then that would be a win-win… surely. To my surprise the outcome I was expecting was not the case.

To be fair, assigning groups randomly had varying levels of success over the years, but experience has taught me that successful collaboration is dependent on a number of factors, and I learned to reflect as well as ask myself a list of questions about my lesson:

- How challenging was the task or activity?
- How much fun did the students perceive the task to be?
- What appeared to be the ability range within the group?
- Did an outright leader emerge within the group?
- What were the levels of individual motivation in the groups?

As we know, it's worth remembering here that the motivation of the learner can be influenced by so many factors on a day-to-day basis, factors out of the teacher's control. For me, the principle here is accepting such a challenge, and learning to manage it within each lesson.

Now, instead of creating teacher-assigned groups randomly I am purposeful in my creation and selection of each group. At the beginning of the academic year, I use a two-week induction period to get to know my post-16 students. The students engage in a variety of activities to both assess their skills and build their confidence, whilst I observe and make mental notes. For me to understand the different personalities within the class, and also to see which group dynamics are working the best, I trial the randomly assigned groups within the two-week period continuously instead of over the year. I use this period to establish a solid foundation with my students of what the learning culture within our classroom should be, and ensure it is an inclusive discovery session of the whole group's expectations – by that I mean the teacher's, the students' and peer-to-peer expectations.

I want my students to visualise what I mean by collaboration; and I start the year by showing my students the end goal. I use the analogy of two athletes who are teammates and train together but at competition on the track they are rivals and compete against each other. This is a visual representation of the classroom (training) and the real world where they may apply for the same jobs and be in competition with each other.

When I gather data and evidence from the two-week induction I create 'learning teams', which are the groups of four to five students that I believe will collaborate most effectively. The learning teams are composed of learners of mixed ability and gender (sometimes I ensure that students from a previous school are separated also). The learning teams would always boil down to the following composition of students:

- One who has performed high on the initial diagnostic assessment. This wouldn't always be the student with the highest average GCSE score but it could be used as an indicator
- One who has not performed well in the two-week induction period and will need motivating and some support. This student wouldn't always have the lowest average GCSE score but it could be used as an indicator
- One student who has demonstrated leadership qualities within the activities set so far
- One student eager to learn new things and who is motivated

If I said that once the learning teams were formed it was an exact science and moving forward the students collaborated effectively forever after, I would be lying. However, it is a great starting point; and like everything in teaching it is an ever evolving and fluid process that allows change and welcomes adaptations to make improvements. The learning teams approach has definitely helped me get to a place of effective collaboration much faster than in my early teaching years, and it is an approach that I continue to use and fine tune.

SOCIAL MEDIA

Join the conversation by using the hashtag #myteachingroutine on social media. Share with other educators how you undertake collaborative learning within your classroom. You can showcase your example through a photo, video, presentation slide or post.

CHAPTER 6
[CONSOLIDATE]

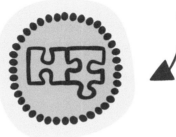

 Learning is not solely about reaching a destination, it's about the experience, journey and reflection. - Mark Martin

OVERVIEW

THIS CHAPTER EXPLORES THE FOLLOWING IDEAS:

* CROSS-REFERENCING THE LESSON OBJECTIVES AND LEARNING OUTCOMES HELPS LEARNERS TO STAY FOCUSED
* EXPLAINING THE KEYWORDS IN DEPTH PROVIDES GREATER CONTEXT FOR REFLECTION
* TEACHERS PAUSING FOR AT LEAST THREE SECONDS HAS A POSITIVE IMPACT ON LEARNING
* HOW TO HELP LEARNERS TO MOVE INFORMATION FROM THEIR SHORT-TERM MEMORY TO LONG-TERM MEMORY

Consolidation can take many forms, such as questioning, mini quizzes, end of lesson summary, etc. It normally happens at the end of an activity or at the end of a lesson. It is a time in the lesson where learners reflect on the content they have learned. The aim is to help learners reflect, summarise and draw together the key concepts they will need to build on in the next stage of learning or in the following lessons. Using an effective technique for consolidation is an additional tool that gives the teacher the opportunity to check the learners' understanding, root out any misconceptions, and assess any progress they have made.

A popular consolidation activity used by teachers is the plenary, which encourages learners to explore and extend their learning (Fisher, 2002). In its simplest form, a plenary asks the question: what has the learner learned in the lesson? To draw parallels with consolidation in other professional fields, I'm always intrigued by athletes and their critique on their strengths and weaknesses. Usain Bolt, the fastest human in the world, once stated, 'There are better starters than me, but I'm a strong finisher.' He had identified his weakness and understood his strength in a race. Throughout his career he would spend extra time training, eating the right food and improving his track time. He then went on to break world records and win eight Olympic gold medals. Most people looking from the outside may have thought this was an easy routine. In one of his post race interviews Bolt stated:

> I think a lot of people, they see you run and they say, 'Ah, it looks so easy, looks effortless.' But before it gets to that point, it's hard; it's hard work. It's a day-in, day-out sacrifice. Just dying this time when you run and you just want to stop, you want to give up, you just want to go home (Thiran, 2018).

Usain Bolt's journey reminds me of our challenge in education to help learners develop reflective and critical thinking that enhances their metacognitive awareness. It's not how they start their learning journey, but how they finish it and whether they are regularly given the opportunity to reflect and understand their own thinking processes.

This level of scrutiny can be seen in critical thinking, which is the thinking behind the answer which leads to deciding what to believe or do. For example, if learners believe they are going to do well in the subject all they need to do is identify their strengths and weaknesses. In comparison, if the learners believe they are not going to do well in the subject they form blind spots in their own ability. Promoting critical thinking in your lesson, though ideal and desirable, is not simple to execute because not every learner acknowledges their academic ability in the same way. This means when introducing the concept it needs to be done through a scheme of work and intervals in a lesson.

The worst time is at the end of the lesson with a few seconds to spare because not all the learners are fully engaged or reflective. Also, the keen learners may 'shout out' the answers or summarise the lesson content thus blocking the opportunity for most of the class to participate readily in the consolidation activity. When implementing thinking critically into your lesson it can be done by employing multiple choice, hinge and random questions to test the understanding of individual learners.

Let me end this section by asserting that there is a practical way of consolidating learning by getting the learners to test out their new skills, language acquired or knowledge they have gained in the task or lesson; this practical way is through critical thinking. This method of application is transferable and with some experience the learner can apply their new skills to everyday activities.

 HINTS & TIPS

1. End the lesson with one minute's silence
2. Get learners to log their blind spots, misconceptions and errors for further reflection and discussion
3. Provide opportunities for further discussion either after the lesson, or in homework or the VLE
4. Challenge thinking through focused questioning

ENDING A LESSON

When ending a lesson, a plenary is normally used to review the aims and consolidate the learners' learning. It's the part of the lesson where learners reflect on what they have learned and accomplished. For plenaries to be effective teachers need to spend some time planning activities to either recall or demonstrate what they have learned during the lesson. Fisher (2002) identifies three main intentions of summarising learners' work at the lesson's end:

*   The first intention is to prompt learners to give answers and explain how they got to the conclusion and the skills they needed to use
*   The second intention is to monitor and observe the learners' response and ensure they have developed and can use the appropriate language
*   The third intention is to encourage the learner to connect their learning to the broader topic and area of the curriculum

Also it's important for learners to understand what progress they have made. The common mistake teachers make is not leaving enough time for the plenary to take place or make it meaningful. To end the lesson effectively it is highly recommended the teacher has a range of different strategies in their portfolio. These strategies may include:

*   Recapping the lesson's content
*   Providing feedback on the classwork
*   Challenging thinking through focused questioning
*   Providing opportunities for further discussion either after the lesson or for homework

I would also state that a well-balanced plenary or end of lesson activity should engage all learners, establish a reasonable pace so learners can process the activity and provide a challenge on any topic or misconception. The aim is for the learner to access a deeper learning of the work which can be extended beyond the classroom. I must emphasise that if the plenary is not well thought through it could allow learners to go off task or cause disruptions.

RECALLING INFORMATION

Have you ever attended an event and had a great conversation with a person in which you learned a lot, but then you managed to forget their name? There are various methods that can assist you to recall the details of the conversation, but more importantly, the person's name. This is similar for our learners who can recall elements of a topic but forget key details and, as a result, may end up performing poorly in an assignment, test or real world application.

Recalling information can be linked with cognitive psychology, which examines the interpretative behaviour and observational methods we use as we attempt and complete tasks daily: for example, the activities we do every day without stopping to think about the complexity of the task such as using a controller to play a computer game. Learning a new skill can be broken down into four stages of competence. The theory was initially founded by Martin M. Broadwell back in 1969 (Broadwell, 1969). In the 1970s, Noel Burch from Gorrdon Training International coined the theory 'the four phases for learning new skills'. I refer to the four stages of competence and add what psychologists now consider to be the final stage, as follows:

Unconscious incompetence (ignorance)

The learner is not aware of the skill or relevance of the skill area. The learner must become conscious of their incompetence before development of the new skill or learning can begin. Teachers normally use a range of methods to help learners understand their ability and how they can apply it to their education and the real world.

Conscious incompetence (learning)

The learner acknowledges the skill but doesn't know how to apply it correctly to different tasks or challenges. Also they understand their weaknesses and what they need to do to practise the skill. The teacher may provide practice tasks for the learner to do in order to improve their ability; it's down to the learner to put in the time and effort to practise the skill, while the teacher creates the space for them to do so.

Conscious competence (learning)

The learner can use the skill but needs to think in order to use it. For the learner to move onto the next stage they need to practise the skill until it becomes 'automatic' or 'second nature'. The teacher might not intervene as the learner can use the skills with minimal assistance. So the feedback given to the learner needs to be constructive and relevant for them to excel in their learning.

Unconscious competence (mastery)

The learner already has practised the skills until it becomes 'second nature' or 'automatic'. For example typing on a keyboard or playing a sport. At this point the learner can complete the task with confidence, precision and relevance. Teachers will encourage the learner to maintain, refine or enhance those skills so they don't forget or slack when applying them to a given situation.

Reflective competence (continual)

This stage is additional. This is where the learner keeps on reflecting on their skills so bad habits or blind spots don't creep in and displace their ability. Continual reflection and development commits the learner to lifelong learning and not just a moment in the classroom. Teachers can get learners to use their skills to solve a problem in their local area or community, then support the learner to write their work up in their CV or professional portfolio. Frankly, this is a good stage for all learners, including teachers, so that we can reflect on our thinking and learning and not be afraid to de-bias and move forward in our learning if we have to.

These stages of competence are heavily linked to cognitive learning, which is learning how to learn, developing a true understanding of the content beyond memorisation and repetition (Kirschner and Hendrick, 2020). Helping learners to understand their thought processes in recalling information is challenging but a very useful skill to learn. Once learners identify and become comfortable with a preferred style (e.g. mind maps, retrieval questions, flash cards) of recalling information then the next step would be for the learner to use these methods in lessons, and most importantly, in applying them to their work. However it's also important to encourage learners to go beyond a preferred style and embrace other styles as they encounter more in their learning journey. Using this consolidation technique is not solely checking the learners' understanding but also offering them skills to go away and continue recalling information from the content covered and learned in the lesson. Teachers may even use what is termed 'spaced learning': the separation of learning skills or concepts over more than one lesson and usually across a term. The point here is that learners don't stop learning in the class; they use the days or weeks to meditate on the content to perfect their ideas and understanding.

TIMING TO RESPOND

In teaching 'time' is everything: it's the compass to how we start and end our lessons. Time can go slowly if you are under stress or managing a challenging situation, yet it can go very fast when the experience is enjoyable and fun.

- Have you ever thought how long it takes to pour in and draw out knowledge from our learners in, let's say, an hour-long lesson?
- Do we spend the majority of the time pouring in and leaving far less time to draw out?

'Pouring in' can be defined as giving learners knowledge and information to process, whereas 'drawing out' builds on what learners already know or learned in that duration of time. The ratio of pouring in and drawing out will differ depending on the time in the school year as well as on whether an exam is imminent.

How does a teacher know when to pour in and when to draw out so they can maintain the correct focus and have a sense of balance?

This could be measured through using the 20% teacher work rate and 80% learners' work rate ratio. If the teacher is working harder than the learners to disseminate information there is an imbalance.

In the 1980s Mary Budd Rowe explored the term 'wait time', which looked into the amount of time learners should be given to answer a question. Teachers pausing for at least three seconds had a positive impact on learning compared to a one-second pause time. The one-second pause gave the learners no time to process or respond to the question comfortably (Rowe, 1986). The truth is learners need time to retain and process new information, and this newly acquired information is more likely to lead them into a wider world of knowledge and understanding than information being limited to the scope of the course. This level of drawing out requires time, patience and empathy in order to create a foundation for learners to respond appropriately. Teachers should strive to have and maintain good time management, subject knowledge, questioning skills and delivery to eliminate a pressurised atmosphere for the learner. The teacher should read the room, look at the body language of each learner, and listen to their conversations; and here listening means noticing the tone, pace, word choice, and even non-fluency features like hesitation, repetition, etc.

When it comes to the questioning and answering segment of the lesson, adopt the method of selecting learners to contribute, rather than waiting for learners to put up their hand; so then no one gets to hide or shy away from answering the questions. If learners get the question wrong, keep the dialogue open without giving away the answer. You may want to rephrase the question or even have a brief discussion around the said response:

Let's unpack learner X's statement further to see if there are ways that we can develop it?

TIMING TO RESPOND

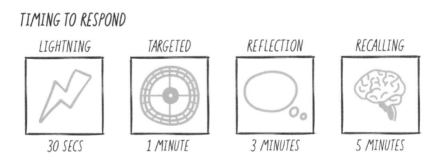

LIGHTNING	TARGETED	REFLECTION	RECALLING
30 SECS	1 MINUTE	3 MINUTES	5 MINUTES

There is another way you could approach the situation, by waiting between 30 seconds and a minute before selecting a learner to answer the questions. This gives the whole class the opportunity to think and reflect on the question in silence or write down possible responses. The benefits of having a moment of stillness helps improve their focus, trigger their long-term memory and reduce stress levels. To implement wait time in your classes use your watch or display a countdown timer on the board so learners can visualise a timer/clock and see they have sufficient time to respond. The cardinal rule is that you should give learners sufficient time and not rush them when asking questions. If you do fall into the habit of moving on regardless of how learners respond that will define future engagements.

SHORT-TERM TO LONG-TERM MEMORY

Supporting learners to recall what they have learned last lesson, last week or last term is a challenging task. Helping learners to categorise information and move it into long-term memory, where it's stored in knowledge structures, is the ambition. Just like a filing cabinet you need to ensure the files are labelled correctly and information can be retrieved when requested. The efficiency of the filing cabinet is based on the way it's been designed and maintained over a period of time. The filing cabinet may come under inspection to see if the information exists within the specific sections and information being retrieved is accurate. Not only does a teacher need to have a strong grasp of the subject or subject knowledge, they should seek to help learners organise their learning.

Consolidating the learning is much more than a five-minute activity at the end of the lesson; consolidation is an indication to the teacher of what is being retained in the short- and long-term memory. Teachers need to avoid going off task, overloading the learner with excess information, or providing weak explanations. This can be mitigated if teachers are aware of Cognitive Load Theory, which explores the amount of information that working or short-term memory can hold at one time, much in the same way that having too many tabs on your web browser slows down the performance and impedes user experience. To keep the browser working at an optimal level, it's essential to close all tabs not in use. Then create a folder to save web pages or bookmark them, so they can be retrieved in the future. Similarly, for learners to perform at the optimal level, it is about helping them to transfer new information from the working memory into the long-term memory.

The teacher's role is to create an environment that reduces unnecessary distractions and barriers in order to access the content. The onus is on the teacher to ensure their content, instructions and questioning are relevant and centred around the topic. I can remember marking Year 10 computer science exam papers and the majority of the learners had got a particular question wrong because they had confused the topic with another concept. I was mystified why they all had given similar incorrect responses; I tried to reflect on the lesson and the method I had taken to deliver the content. A few questions came to mind:

- Did I cover this topic mentioning other concepts? This might have been confusing for learners.
- Did I cover the topic quickly and move onto another concept without checking they fully understood the content?
- Did I need to teach the topics separately to avoid any confusion with other concepts?

I think if I had another opportunity to deliver the content I would:

- Ensure presentation slides have enough information to define the topic;
- Avoid any exaggerated examples that connect the topic to another concept;
- Use the ADEPT (Analogy, Diagram, Example, Plain-English description, and then Technical description) model;
- Get learners to write a summary of the topic covered to check for and root out any misunderstandings;
- Give learners the chance to retrieve knowledge that they might have begun to forget through revisiting topics on a frequent basis, focused revision (spaced practice) and low stakes questioning.

LESSON OBJECTIVES CHECKLIST

The consolidation part of the lesson needs to comprise carefully planned tasks, be well paced, and for the most part engaging. Some teachers will use the lesson objectives as a checklist for learners to review what task or activity they have completed. The next step would be for the learners to show their competencies by completing a specific task to demonstrate, explain, or apply their knowledge and this might be differentiated by the language and terminology that learners are expected to use. The lesson objectives checklist allows the learner to know how far they have progressed in the lesson.

At the end of my Year 10 computer science class, I got learners to review their work using the lesson objectives checklist criteria. They had to give a level for their progress and effort. I then got their peers to verify their mark and make any necessary comments. This exercise was useful in getting learners to reflect on their work and involve their peers in the process and became very effective when I made it a permanent feature to every end of lesson over a term. Learners needed sufficient time to complete the checklist, so I had to be disciplined to make time in the lesson for learners to complete it. I also got learners to review the information they had put on the checklist at the beginning of the lesson so they could continue to build on the previous lesson.

There are other ways the lesson objectives could be used, for example allowing learners to rank the difficulty of the objective or how they felt completing the activity by drawing a happy or sad face. Also you could get learners to write down two or three questions related to the lesson objective that they would like to ask their peers in the classroom. This helps the learner to critically think about the content they have covered in the lesson, which will then extend and deepen their learning by using their soft skills to interact with others. The aim here is to get learners to be the key contributors in their learning; it should not just be another exercise to kill time when there appear to be the odd spare minutes at the end of the lesson. To make this a consistent feature in your lesson, you could add a tracker system where learners write down what objective they have completed and whether they can apply it to another task.

In my Year 10 computer science class I would stop the lesson 10 minutes before the end and get learners to review the lesson objectives. Some learners would tick all the boxes to rush through the activity or they would not be accurate in how they measured their progress. So I decided to link each lesson objective with an exam question, so they could not just rush through the process. The outcomes were interesting: some learners returned to the lesson's task to review their answers, and some learners used the textbook to check their understanding. Having the checklist created a learning dialogue with different learners, with the aim of rooting out any misconceptions or reducing the gaps in the learners' understanding. The experience taught me not to underestimate the thinking time given for learners to understand their own learning progress and the importance of learners seeing themselves as reviewers of their own learning.

EXPLAIN THE KEYWORDS

Similar to the lesson objectives checklist there are certain keywords learners will need to know before the end of specific lessons. I would normally leave the keywords on the board so learners can clearly see what words have been highlighted, hear the pronunciation of the words, and show an example of how they are written in a sentence in an assignment or in an examination response. Normally, I tell my learners, it's not simply a case of defining the keyword but having the ability to apply it, adapt it and scrutinise information. Then, I get learners to unpack the keywords by using a mind map to see the connection between the different aspects of the topic. The next part of the activity is to get the learners to explain what they understand of the keywords or about associations with these key-words. Random learners are selected to explain what the keywords mean. They have the option to select the keyword or allow their peer to select one for them. The rest of the class will monitor the response and highlight any areas for correction or further explanation. The learners that struggle with the keywords are given the full definitions, so they can follow along and cross-check their peers' explanations. This always created a buzz in the classroom because some of their peers would give them the odd wink or whispering hints which led them to remember the keywords. Creating an enjoyable element around the keywords wasn't just about getting learners prepared for the test, but also for long-term learning. Getting them to retain information over a long period of time and apply-ing that information to the real world beyond the exam is where magic happens.

For this to work and be sustained I needed to create space for learners to come to lessons with practical examples of the keywords used in everyday interactions. So I created a homework activity where learners had to go home and teach three people in their family about the keywords and write a short summary of the conversation. This was extremely powerful because learners were not only generating a dialogue outside the classroom, they were upskilling their family members on the topic. The impact was immense because whenever the topic and keywords arose, learners would refer back to teaching their relatives or provide real examples of the keywords being used in their lives. This was highlighted when I taught a module on cyber security and learners needed to learn the different types of computer vulnerabilities. Learners were given a homework activity to inform their families about the dangers online using the keywords learned in lessons. The following lesson learners came back with examples of their family members being victims to online fraud and were able to correctly use the keywords (i.e. phishing) to describe the situation. I then started to see learners using these examples in their exams to illustrate how computer systems can become compromised. The big takeaway from using keywords is that you have to make them come alive so learners are encouraged to store them in their long-term memory and apply them to appropriate situations. The more creative you are in helping learners to use the keywords beyond the scope of the lesson, the more it will support them in linking the keywords to the real world.

 ## REFLECTION QUESTIONS

- **How do we set our environments for learners to be reflective learners?**
- **Do we give them enough time to be reflective?**
- **Do you plan for reflection throughout your lessons?**

EXPERIENTIAL LEARNING

Experiential learning can be thought of as the process of learning by doing. There is a huge benefit in engaging learners with hands-on experiences and reflection. It allows them to connect theories and knowledge learned in the classroom with the real world. Experiential learning is derived from Kolb's traditional learning cycle (Kolb, 1984), which consists of four stages – experiencing, reflecting, thinking and acting. The approach was originally developed for teams in businesses to solve big internal challenges. But decades later it then trickled into education and the classroom. The transition into education was a good fit because learners don't only focus on what they learn in the classroom or school premises. Learning experiences happen everywhere and with the rise of technology, the internet and mobile phones learners have access to much more information than ever before. They can interact and engage with the world in new and meaningful ways. A prime example is Pokemon Go, the augmented reality mobile app which encourages individuals to find digital creatures in their local areas using GPS technology. The mobile app didn't come with clear set instructions on how to play the game, but as the users immersed themselves in the challenges the rules started to unfold. The extraordinary thing about the game was users dived straight into the challenges, learning from their mistakes and perfecting their gameplay. Pokemon Go illustrated the essence of experiential learning and the benefits of learning by doing.

The approach goes one step further and examines our experiences in relation to our emotions, cognition and environment. These features are sometimes not a factor when it comes to reviewing our learners' learning journey or academic outcomes; the education system mainly focuses on studying for an exam.

Experiential learning goes beyond the surface learning and focuses on deep learning through practical activities, experimenting and role playing. Introducing this method into the classroom with a focus on consolidating the learning can help learners understand what they're learning by their efforts in applying and discussing concepts rather than just memorising them. A group of learners volunteered to build a games PC for the after-school club. I was amazed by their expertise and knowledge when it came to building the PC from scratch. I asked them, 'Who taught you how to build a PC?' They all laughed and said YouTube. They had sourced all of the parts of the PC and knew how it would perform with some of their favourite games. This experience taught me that when learners have a purpose and passion it leads to greater productivity.

In every school I've worked in, I get learners who randomly approach me to talk about their hobbies and interests outside of school. These range from building servers to playing online games. You can hear the passion in their voice, and instead of shutting them down I try to explore how I can connect their interests to the curriculum and potential career paths. So I decided to set up an esports room in my school based in South London to help learners aged between 14 and 19 understand that the soft skills they are using to play online games are the same skills needed to get a job and navigate the real world. I stuck the soft skills words around the esports room. The fascinating thing was learners started to have technical conversations based around the esports room. I then tried to help them transfer the knowledge and use those identical technical conversations when it came to understanding different parts of their classwork and behaviour around the school. For experiential learning to work effectively there needs to be wider support from school leaders, community and industry because with their help they can empower teachers and learners to use their skills learned beyond the curriculum. The difficulty is the time needed to connect with the industry and how you work with them effectively.

My best advice is to connect with companies through their professional online profiles, attend industry events and invite them to your school. Also be intentional with your ask and get them to see your learners in action. I normally prepped my learners with several questions to ask when an important person from an industry is visiting the school. When the visitor stepped into the class the learners quickly threw up their hands to greet them and explore what they do. There was one occasion where my learners explained to my guest how technology would change the landscape in the next 20 years. The visitor was not only surprised, he wanted to get these learners in front of his colleagues to share their insights.

PERSONAL EXPERIENCE

In my initial teacher training and during the first few years of teaching there was no mention of how the brain works and the impact it has on learning. The more I attended external personal development sessions on brain training and saw other educators around the world post their work on social media, the more I started to see the benefits this can have on learners and the learning environment. However, I wasn't clear how I could embed these techniques into my lessons until I met a colleague who was using a range of different techniques (i.e. spacing, distributed practice and interleaved practice) in their lesson. They advised me to use these techniques to break the lesson down into small steps and limit the amount of information on my presentation slides. The starter activity should allow learners to retrieve the information they learned in the last lesson. The aim of the starter activity was for learners to build confidence in assessing their long-term memory. The next step was to put several hinge questions into the activity so I could see how learners were processing the information. The colleague also encouraged me to produce examples of what good retrieval practice should look like and get learners to see the process. This is something I never thought of doing. Normally, I would set the work and assume learners should attempt the work before showing them a structure of retrieving information. However, providing learners time to reflect, recap and review their work gave me a unique insight into how they were grasping new concepts. While I thought I was doing well in teaching and delivering the scheme of work, the learners were having a mixed learning experience. Some were excelling in the lesson but some were struggling to keep up with my teaching approach. So having that time at the end of the lesson to check what learners had retained or learned was a good indication for me to root out any misconceptions or tailor my delivery. My colleague's input had significantly enhanced my practice and showed me the benefits of working with others. Also the school allowed me to do a risk lesson (which gives teachers the opportunity to teach a lesson underpinned by academic research or good practice) and then share the experience with other colleagues within the department. These interventions gave me the confidence and experience to see how consolidating a lesson can be done with a focus on short-term and long-term memory testing.

However, there is no perfect formula to consolidating a lesson because every school system is different and subjects have different requirements. The main takeaway is to understand the different methods you can use to consolidate learning and appreciate how the brain works in retrieving and processing information. Also, consolidating shouldn't only be seen as helping learners memorise information for an exam but also as helping them understand how they can use skills in different situations and in the outside world.

ANOTHER TEACHER'S EXPERIENCE: BUKKY YUSUF (SENIOR LEADER, SCIENCE LEAD, EDUCATIONAL CONSULTANT)

I have always loved teaching. Right from the time when I was a teacher volunteer many years ago until today. That said, what I struggled with for many years were the ways in which I could meaningfully end the lesson. The plenary was something that I really needed to craft and work upon. It wasn't that I was unaware about the need to end the lesson in a formal way. What made it difficult was looking at ways that helped students to clearly reveal what they had learnt. A 2004 report, as part of an evaluation of the implementation of the Key Stage 3 Strategy Pilot, highlighted Ofsted's finding 'that plenaries … are not allocated enough time and are often the weakest part of the lesson' (Department for Education and Skills, 2004: 4). I was not alone with this particular struggle. I can still remember the time during my PGCE that I excitedly shared the plenary I had created for the lesson that I had taught. My tutor noted how visual it was however they then pointed out that it lacked challenge and did not allow students to apply their new learning. In addition to that, I struggled to ensure that I provided enough time for students to review their learning during the plenary. It would be a number of years before I crafted plenaries that enabled students to apply their newly acquired knowledge, skills and included metacognition opportunities. I also learnt that in order to get students to effectively review their learning, it had to be planned. I could not just wing it.

STUDENTS' OPTIONS WHEN CONSOLIDATING THEIR WORK

Learned	Still didn't understand	Question posed to the teacher
Reflective moment		

So I moved from plenaries that got students to summarise what they had learnt in one sentence, to a review of questions where students noted things they learnt/still didn't understand/a question they posed to me, to lengthy reflection questions which got students to reflect upon their knowledge and skill. In addition to all the research about the purposes of a plenary, I use the plenary to boost a student's confidence by providing a problem they were unable to answer at the start of the lesson and for them to show me how they can now do it. Using an exam question during the plenary is a powerful way to do this. The plenary activity allows the students to see how much they have progressed (or identify what students can now do as a result of the lesson in relation to the learning outcomes). This then informs what I will plan/teach in the next sequence of lessons, thereby making it a significant part of the lesson.

My takeaway points regarding a plenary:

1. In order for this to be effective, you need to plan what will be done in the plenary.
2. The plenary can help students to review and demonstrate their learning (in terms of knowledge/skills/application).
3. Meaningful plenary activities can help inform your lesson planning.

SOCIAL MEDIA

Join the conversation by using the hashtag #myteachingroutine on social media. Share with other educators how you consolidate learning within your lessons. You can showcase your example through a photo, video, presentation slide or post.

CHAPTER 7

[REFLECT]

 Your greatest tool to knowing your worth and impact in the classroom is being able to reflect. - Mark Martin

OVERVIEW

THIS CHAPTER EXPLORES THE FOLLOWING IDEAS:

* TAKING TIME OUT TO REVIEW YOUR PROGRESS IN THE CLASSROOM IS PRICELESS
* COLLEAGUES CAN PROVIDE CONSTRUCTIVE FEEDBACK ON YOUR TEACHING
* WE SHOULD BE OPEN TO CHANGE AND DOING THINGS DIFFERENTLY
* WHAT WORKS FOR YOU SHOULD BE SHARED WITH OTHER TEACHERS

I have added a bonus chapter here to help you digest the different stages within the book and an opportunity for you to review your teaching routine, which means reflecting on your own practice. Every teaching routine has a sell by date and potency. It's like having a new year's resolution which you are excited to follow until the novelty runs out. How do you motivate yourself and bring consistency to your practice throughout the school term?

As we are in reflection mode… Why are you teaching, and why do you teach the way that you teach? Is it an effective way to teach for all of your learners? Are you progressing in your teaching or is there a sense of being on a treadmill as you simply get through week after week and half term after half term? What is informing you to be the best version of yourself and your teaching routine?

Working in education is one of the most rewarding careers in the world. Understanding where you are presently and where you are going will help you to refine your teaching routine and what you do in the classroom; and refine them consistently without seeing it as a burden. And, let me add, there is a sense of irony here. A routine – a 'customary course of action or more or less mechanical performance' (www.etymonline.com), or a beaten path – wouldn't require review and reflection because it serves some purpose, and I get that; however, there will always be a need to consider who a teacher has to communicate with, why there will be a need to communicate to your learners, when, in what space, and how you communicate. The list goes on and a greater sense of who, why and how will come into sharper focus. So routine and reflection for improvement do appear paradoxical.

As already mentioned in this book, a lot of academic literature puts learners at the heart of the discourse and leaves teachers' discourse on the periphery. I want to promote this chapter of the book as a shout to put the wellbeing of teachers at the centre of the narrative, so that we can reflect and put up a mirror to ourselves. Teachers have a lot of responsibilities in and out of the classroom; this sometimes can consume their time to be creative and innovative. I can't emphasise more strongly, don't give up your effort to learn new ways of teaching and remain curious in your practice.

Learning around your subject and adopting an attitude of creative curiosity can be infectious and influence your learners, giving them a sense of confidence in how and why they learn new things. We know that keeping ourselves positive and focused on our teaching routine is challenging. The tick box culture in schools which expects teachers to be outstanding all the time keeps many naturally creative teachers in their comfort zone and risk averse to trying anything new. It keeps teachers safe and yet at the same time restricts them from being outstanding through over-using fixed and familiar methods. The constant reminders from school leaders about improving exam results, pushing up the league table, and a looming school inspection have ways of keeping teachers from rocking the boat, causing unnecessary pressure and amassing workload on themselves. This cocktail from school leaders can cause both anxiety and fear. My main mantra is to define yourself before you let the education system define you.

REFLECTIVE TEACHING

Reflective teaching is being able to assess how well you are performing in your classroom. It is much more than looking at test results or student progression. It delves into what is and isn't working in your teaching practice and prompts you to make the necessary changes. An example of this is doing a SWOT analysis on your practice, which will give you an overview of your delivery. This informal diagnostic can be done on your own or with a colleague.

In seeking constructive feedback from learners or colleagues you might ask a colleague to observe you, create a learner survey to gather feedback, or give a risk lesson which requires you to try something new. Whatever you decide to do you need to ask yourself what you learned from the experience and what effect it had on your learners. Now it's important to state what works today may not work tomorrow. Being reflective is a continual process, which requires you to be critical of your practice but with the clear distinction of not being hard on yourself.

There are three types of colleagues I would normally seek out to help me reflect on my practice:

New teacher: This teacher is likely to be enthusiastic, full of energy, and loves to try new things in their classroom because they would have recently completed their teacher training. These individuals are receptive to new advice and feedback. They also help you to reflect on the mistakes you made in their position and what things they should avoid.

Accountable teacher: This teacher is in a similar role, age group or shares similar experiences. As you both have a similar understanding of the education field and demands, you can be open and honest with each other. These individuals are able to tell when things are going well or badly. Through listening to their advice they help you to reflect and challenge any areas of weakness.

Wise teacher: This teacher has been in the profession for several decades and has seen many changes and been through many transitions. Their wisdom helps you to reflect, ponder and question the things you do in the classroom. These individuals can offer lots of sound advice which helps in your being the best version of yourself.

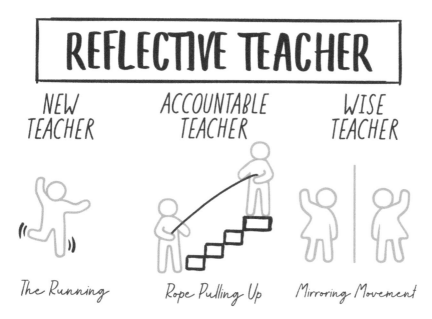

REFLECTIVE TEACHER

NEW TEACHER — ACCOUNTABLE TEACHER — WISE TEACHER

The Running — Rope Pulling Up — Mirroring Movement

THE REFLECTIVE CYCLE

We are familiar with the term 'lifelong learner', but we should also be 'lifelong practitioners' who are conscious of the impact we are making in and out of the classroom. There are many questions that come to mind as a practitioner, for example,

- How do we continually refine our teaching practice and be relevant in an ever changing landscape?
- Is this new classroom method driven by research, good practice or school/government policy?
- Are we doing this for our professional development or just to tick a box?
- If I get outstanding results in my classroom, why should I be concerned about these new pedagogies?

The reason why these questions keep popping up is because the teacher's professional development is rarely personalised or differentiated. Also there is a big difference between a graduate teacher and a teacher with 10+ years' experience. More needs to be done to support teachers to become experts in their subject or specialism. I made the effort to find time after school or on the weekend to upskill in my subject area. It paid off in ways I never imagined because it gave me a bird's eye view of my curriculum and new ways I could use my skill sets. It had a significant impact on my mental health and wellbeing knowing I was being empowered to become an advanced skilled teacher in my subject area. Unfortunately, for many schools the CPD programme is tailored towards meeting the government's inspection framework or school's teaching and learning requirements.

In my years of experience the best teachers I've met are the ones that are the most creative and innovative in the classroom. These individuals can be utilised within the school to share their work or lead on professional development throughout the school or department. However, to help teachers take risks, be more creative and innovative in their practice school leaders need to give them sufficient time to implement new strategies in their classroom, setting up multidisciplinary initiatives to get teachers working together across departments and allowing teachers to take part in action research. It would be great to see more schools advocating research-led approaches within their local context rather than what's trending in the educational sphere.

The reflective cycle is not one thing – it consists of many things that teachers need to do in order to be effective within the classroom. It requires reflection, training, support and encouragement.

 HINTS & TIPS

1. **Try and monitor your performance with a diary of what went well (WWW) and even better if (EBI)**
2. **Look into new academic research on how the brain functions**
3. **When you reflect on school matters make sure you are conscious of mental health and wellbeing**
4. **Make safe spaces for you to reflect with colleagues**

REFLECTION QUESTIONS

- Have you explored research on being a reflective teacher?
- When do you reflect on your practice? At the start or end of the week?
- Do you have a diary or log so you can review your performance over a period of time?
- How can you make your classroom more inclusive?

REAL LIFE EXPERIENCE

Several years ago I wanted to define myself as an edu-innovator, which meant I wanted to bring new tech and approaches into my teaching practice. My colleagues laughed at me and told me to focus on my teaching practice and avoid doing anything different that would amount to me wasting my time. I am someone who considers any criticism, and believe that sometimes you have to test the criticism to see if it is valid or not.

I thought if what my colleagues were saying was true then I had to take their feedback on board and change my perspective about bringing new tech and approaches into my teaching. In other words, I had to say no to innovation in my teaching or in my classroom. The truth was that my bemused colleagues were wrong and myopic because I was getting positive feedback from lesson observations and good comments from other tech teachers in different schools. I knew I was onto something but I had to take a risk beyond the norms of my department.

My determination to do things differently could be considered to be a crazy move especially when you've got a family, bills to pay and other responsibilities. I could see why it was easier to conform and keep things simple – it was less hassle. But I didn't join the profession to fit in, but to stand out. My approach to education led me to travel to different countries to share my work and vision. But I must admit it did take a serious amount of reflecting and drowning out the negative thoughts of failing.

The challenge

The challenge to be authentic and original was not to be moulded into a role imposed by a myopic mentor, a strict academised system, or even a role restricted by past thoughts on how teachers taught in the past. It is easy to submit to fear and conform rather than adopt a creative curiosity and know when and how to resist what is imposed by political bystanders – here I mean social commentators, politicians and ill-informed journalists and those who have no real experience of teaching under stressful conditions.

Being professional and simultaneously curiously creative in the face of stress is to be respected. Arsène Wenger, who was an unconventional genesis and rise to football management, articulates the sentiment like this: 'I had infinite respect for the players: the ones who had a philosophy of the game, who favoured individual expression, who were not afraid to fight and confront their fears, rather than submit to them' (Wenger, 2020: 44).

Another pioneer was Ray Kroc, the American businessman who purchased McDonald's in the early 1960s and is credited with the company's global expansion, and was always open to new possibilities. He was known to say, 'As long as you're green you're growing: as soon as you're ripe you start to rot' (Robson, 2020: 99).

Despite the challenges you can still be innovative and push the boundaries of what you are doing in your classroom. Let's continue to put teachers first and give them time to upskill, introduce new techniques into their lessons and acknowledge their efforts. This can be achieved by setting up internal and external knowledge transfer networks where teachers get the opportunity to share good practice and proven research.

PERSONAL EXPERIENCE

I tend to do a lot of thinking and reflecting on my teaching and learning journey. Many people ask me when my pivotal moment in the classroom happened. I think it was when the UK's Department for Education changed the digital skills curriculum from Information Communication Technology to computer science in 2014. The ICT curriculum taught learners how to drive a car whilst the computer science curriculum taught learners how to put the car together.

This meant I had to upskill myself to deliver this new curriculum and ensure learners made reasonable progress. The ICT curriculum was predominately project based and the new computer science curriculum is exam based. As a result the pressure to prepare learners for an exam was immense. My teaching style needed to change from checking learners' practical skills to helping learners memorise content for an end of course exam. I was out of my comfort zone, and totally so because I was used to helping learners unlock their digital skills, but now I was helping them to retain information over a long period of time.

This major change required me to learn new concepts, theories and information in computer science. Firstly, I had to review my ability to teach the course, seek CPD and ask for help in understanding some of the terminologies. This helped me to be more open about my teaching practice than previously, mainly because I didn't want to get things wrong. It can be difficult to be critical about your own work, being honest with yourself and knowing your weaknesses.

However, being a positive reflective teacher helps you not take yourself too seriously, become less defensive over your work, and not channel feelings of shame or weakness when asking for help. The aim of reflecting is to bring you to a greater understanding of your interactions with learners and to keep on refining your approach to teaching. There is no silver bullet to reflecting on your teaching, but it requires continual review through peer observation, writing logs, learners' feedback, training and talking with others.

ANOTHER TEACHER'S EXPERIENCE: DAVE MARTIN (ENGLISH STUDIES TEACHER)

Loosely speaking I reflect on my teaching, the lesson, engagement with the teaching and learning in a range of spaces – be it rushing down a corridor, on the journey home, when preparing the following lesson with the group, and in/with discussions with other teachers and even the learners. There is no limit to how and when we reflect, is there? Surely reflecting is a thought process, isn't it?

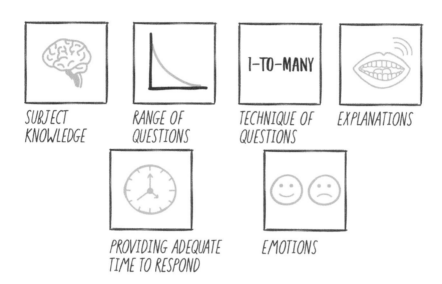

When I reflect, I begin with the state of my emotions, and I'm not suggesting that is the only place to start. I ask, what was my mood during the beginning, the middle, and the ending stages of the lesson? Did I manage my emotion(s) throughout my time with these learners? How did I use my voice from the first utterance? Was the first utterance a greeting or a command? Was my voice supportive, snappish, or even sarcastic? Another way of saying this is, on balance were my initial words regulatory, or used to foster an environment of learning? Did I listen to my learners? Did I listen to MY voice and imagine being a learner listening to that voice? Who was it that ended up setting the linguistic agenda? Was my lesson plan derailed by a reluctant learner or even derailed by myself? Did I manage, or establish beforehand, how other speakers spoke in the learning space? What address terms did I use when speaking to the group? How did I feel about the lesson when in the lesson, and how do I feel now?

I cannot fail to add the following questions: What preceded the lesson in terms of my physical and mental wellbeing? Had I had enough rest and sleep? Did I get to go to the bathroom and/or did I have to hold my water for another X minutes? Was I in pain? Was I stressed? And am I stressed when I'm trying to reflect on my lesson? Did I have to sort out that pressing something beyond the work? Were my thoughts positive? And, if they were not positive did I allow my non-positive thoughts to influence my decision making?

These are examples of some of the probing questions I explore in the first half of my reflection.

Then I go on to consider whether my subject knowledge was on point. I check whether the range of questions, the technique of questioning, the explanations, and the cultural and diverse references for the makeup of my learners were effective. And I mull over whether I over-talked, and if so, when and why.

No doubt my reflections would consider whether the learners achieved specific learning outcomes, and whether they were engaged throughout the lesson. If not, then why not and what might be done on my part as well as their part to improve learning outcomes and engagement? When I reflect, I consider the day in the week, the week in the term; and I think about the effectiveness of my classroom management in the context of when the lesson took place. Was the lesson and my chosen style of teaching more effective before or after lunch? Was the lesson after a not-so-usual-school-day-incident? And, was that event what most of the learners chose to think about when their focus should have been elsewhere?

I consider the weather and its potential impact on myself as a practitioner and the learners. I recall the physical environment where the lesson took place and ask, was it too congested? Too noisy? Was sound leaking from the classroom and affecting others or was the ambient sound from others leaking into our learning space and affecting us? You know what I mean, when the class next door is watching a video with heightened music or a comedic sequence and the sound leaks into your temporary space for learning… or when that certain teacher goes on a shouting rampage and bellows words that everyone is familiar with. And the question returns, how did I manage these expected and/or unexpected challenges simultaneously maintaining a purposeful teaching and learning environment?

Crucial to my reflection are the following questions: How did the lesson transition(s) go? Did the sound in the classroom shift during the transition(s)? Were there healthy pauses in the lesson? How were the unexpected/expected interruptions dealt with? That's interruptions from late comers and colleagues popping in, to school tours of prospective new senior managers looking in classrooms when live lessons are taking place. What did I do to either keep the learners on task during the interruption or get them back on task after the interruption?

The reflective process varies yet is shaped by how I felt, whether learning took place, the fluency and formation of the teaching and learning sequence, the relationship with learners, how I communicated, and how I managed general communication in the learning space.

Near the end of my reflections I ask, what next? What changes might I need to make? Where do I go, or who do I go to, to begin the changes? And will these changes be permanent or temporary?

With all these questions I remind myself of the need to ensure I have the correct balance between realistic and appropriate reflecting and forward planning with action points; nothing should be done in a frantic sense even after a poorly taught lesson, that's just unhealthy.

In the past I have been too harsh and judgemental on the learners, presented material in a boring and off-handed manner due to being in a poor emotional state, or over-taught (and even skipped through) a part of the lesson, and if on reflection that meant apologising and rebuilding the relationship, working on making the teaching more engaging, and finding the right approach to delivering lesson content, then I had to own my behaviour, take the necessary steps towards doing better, and hold to my personal principle of being a learning-teacher… and measure making those practical improvements.

For my wellbeing, I do not over-think and become paranoid; I do not engage in 'blame-games'. I maintain a positive stance about why I teach, why I joined this profession. It comes down to this, I believe that we – the learners, my supportive colleagues, other invested parties and myself – can work together to achieve positive outcomes, so even if I find through reflection that I need to improve to make things better for the learners – and me – I'm willing to go on that journey and make those changes.

Reflection can be approached through literally writing what Tristine Rainer would call a 'New Diary' – 'a personal book in which creativity, play, and self-therapy interweave, foster, and complement each other'. This new diary approach is a way to promote your voice and enhance 'wholeness and coherence' (Rainer, 1978: 26). As further ways of reflecting on my teaching (and my perceptions of the learning) experience(s), I engage in verbal communication with others, share psychological insights, practise meditation and breathing techniques to restore a sense of balance and calm, even after a good day. I find that a walk with a colleague on the way out of the building can be an opportunity for reflective self-care and supportive wellbeing. Let me be clear here, there should be timetabled spaces for this type of reflection, so again, my point is that a short meaningful conversation can be effective to aid reflection, and support teacher wellbeing. I suggest that we should include *how we are*, and not simply how we performed in an imposed context, and this should be a significant part of our teacher-teaching reflection.

SOCIAL MEDIA

Join the conversation by using the hashtag #myteachingroutine on social media. Share with other educators how you reflect on your practice. You can showcase your example through a photo, video, presentation slide or post.

CONCLUSION

Before my final comments, I want to make a point about the future and then raise a few questions. We cannot say what a distant future classroom will look like and whether the STEM agenda, government policies, and educational discourse will alter the way we approach teaching and learning in schools.

We do not know how much of the curriculum will support some of the biggest environmental, geo-political, and social justice (including the cost-of-living crisis) challenges in the world today. We do know from my teaching routine it will prepare learners and educators for change, for being flexible, and facing challenges with a framework that might even evolve. This framework will offer tools and ideas on navigating the evolution of the classroom. In a sense *My Teaching Routine* is a shared self-reflective schemata that encourages teachers to examine their practice.

Lets zoom out. For many years there has been a vast amount of discussion on whether the current education system is fit for purpose and whether it prepares learners for the outside world.

- Is what we are doing in the classroom effectively preparing learners for the future of work and to be local citizens within their communities?
- Are the skills being taught in school to prepare learners for the next stage in their lives?
- Can teachers tell the difference between educational fads or research proven practice?

So many thought-provoking questions, but is our teaching routine in the classroom building our learners up to succeed and to compete in a global market? Schools are so much more than the 'exam factory' that many spectators think they see when they are looking from the outside in.

Teachers' contributions in and out of the classroom live on for generations; they are the stars in space. Their influence in society is priceless; they are constantly shaping society, one class at a time. But we have to look after our teachers because they are human beings and do have feelings and emotions too. For many teachers the profession can feel like a juggling act, where you have different balls – workload, family life, admin, marking, CPD and performance management. Teachers do so much more than teaching.

Think of all the skills that the average teacher will use in a given day. There would be data crunching; coaching and counselling skills; advertising and public speaking skills through promoting ideas for campaigns; keeping abreast of specification changes and ways of assessing assignments; dealing with parents; dealing with 'naughty' learners; writing accounts of incidents; marking; taking new learners in their classes – and some of these activities without the proper training despite many schools and institutions stating that they hold Investors in People awards. You would wish that a ball could be removed or put aside before being expected to add another ball to the number already in the air. The more balls we juggle should not be regarded as a sign of strength, rather, too many balls in flight leaves less time to focus on why we teach. A burnt out teacher is good to no one. A simple, 'Hello how are you? Do you need support with anything?' can change a teacher's morale.

THE PANDEMIC

The Covid-19 pandemic turned a 200-year-old education system upside down overnight, when schools converted their physical spaces to online spaces. Teachers were required to sit in front of a camera and share knowledge to learners who had their cameras off. This is probably the first time for many teachers where they couldn't read the body language of learners and the emotions on their learner's face or quickly provide one-to-one feedback. The traditional teaching approach was not compatible, which meant teachers couldn't talk for a whole hour into a camera screen. They had to mix up their lesson with short activities and creating group conversations. However some learners couldn't access remote learning because they didn't have a laptop, they had poor or no wi-fi access, or they did not have enough room at home to work. The pandemic revealed to us all that far more intervention is needed throughout the country to reduce the inequalities that exist in the British education system under the current Conservative government – a government that has been in power for more than a decade following educational gains made by the previous Labour government. 'Levelling up' has been shown to be mere chatter and politicising; not enough has been put in place in and out of schools and some learners (by class, by a lack of SEN funding and provision) have been left behind.

MOVING WITH THE TIMES

Who you are as a teacher will and should change over time as the world of education will shift depending on political, financial, and other trends. That is inevitable. When I started my career teaching ICT was in vogue, now things have shifted to computer science trending and being in vogue. Who knows what will emerge next but what I advocate is teachers remain fresh and know growth is crucial. Who knows if schools will have more managers and 'leaders' from non-teaching backgrounds or who have never taught a lesson in a school classroom before? And, how might that affect the world of education? Who knows whether leaders in education will be better trained and encouraged to be better listeners and collaborators with frontline classroom teachers, and together make better decisions for everyone in the world of education – everyone meaning inclusion for the wide abilities and stages of all learners, parents from all socio-economic back-grounds, teachers at all stages in their profession, and the communities that schools and other stakeholders serve?

The hybrid model of online and offline teaching is here to stay, and clearly our teaching routines need to be able to accommodate this style of learning. Emerging technologies provide a real opportunity to enhance the learning experience for our learners. Tech won't replace teachers but it will replace those who are reluctant to use it. Teachers need to continually upskill themselves and understand how technology can be used in their practice to enhance the learning experience for learners.

My best advice is to join teacher learning networks and attend events where teachers share good practice. They help you to work smart, save time and improve areas of weakness. It's not for teachers to abdicate their responsibilities in developing themselves; they have to own their professional development. This book is designed for teachers to revisit and explore the chapters – similar to the sentiment in the introduction to the First Folio of Shakespeare's plays in 1623 which encourages the reader to read over the lines of the plays 'again, and again', to reap more and more understanding of Shakespeare's ideas in the plays. I am no Shakespeare nor is this book like the First Folio of his plays. No, but I suggest that revisiting a text can yield more meaning, and in this case *My Teaching Routine* is designed to be re-read to help us reflect and think about our practice. The end of each chapter points you to the hashtag #myteachingroutine, to encourage you to join the conversation. Also the book was intentionally designed to show different ways of thinking about education, which go beyond the traditional writing of education and western thinking of education. I hope this book inspires you to enhance what you do in and out of the classroom.

There is a relationship between the physical learning environment and learner responses – be they cognitive, socio-emotional, or other physiological responses. The inevitability of change in how buildings are utilised and managed through health and safety regulations, and the use of technology and hands-on equipment in educational spaces have had a predictable impact on the need for institutions to reconsider how our schools are set up, and to ask whether the physical space in buildings is used effectively. The growth in technology has shown that being connected to the internet is essential; and even before the Covid-19 pandemic a lack of access to the internet was deemed to be a sign of poverty. The power of wi-fi, portable digital devices and school VLEs has made learning more accessible anywhere in a school environment. This is important because with the falling cost of using digital technologies, schools will make use of digital platforms for supporting independent learning away from the classroom, and such opportunities should not be ignored. However, the classroom is still the focal point for learning and nurturing learners to achieve greater outcomes in both their academic and personal lives.

SHARE YOUR TEACHING ROUTINE USING THE HASHTAG #MYTEACHINGROUTINE

How do you share your ideas for Connect, Demonstrate, Activate, Facilitate, Collaborate and Consolidate?

REFERENCES

Anderson, L. W. and Krathwohl, D. R. (2001). *A Taxonomy for Learning, Teaching, and Assessing: A Revision of Bloom's Taxonomy of Educational Objectives*. New York: Longman.

Bandura, A. (1977). Self-efficacy: Toward a unifying theory of behavioral change. *Psychological Review*, 84(2), 191–215.

BBC Sounds (2021, 9th July). *Rethink Education: Technology and Education*. Available at: https://www.bbc.co.uk/sounds/play/m000xmyz

Biggs, J. (1999). What the student does: teaching for enhanced learning. *Higher Education Research & Development*, 18(1), 57–75.

Bloom, B. S. (1956). *Taxonomy of Educational Objectives: The Classification of Educational Goals* (1st edn). New York: Longmans, Green.

Broadwell, M. M. (1969). Teaching for Learning (XVI.). *The Gospel Guardian*. Available at: https://www.wordsfitlyspoken.org/gospel_guardian/v20/v20n41p1-3a.html

Burgess, S. and Thomson, D. (2019). *Making the Grade: The Impact of GCSE Reforms on the Attainment Gap between Disadvantaged Pupils and their Peers*. London: Sutton Trust.

Charoensukmongkol, P. (2014). Benefits of mindfulness meditation on emotional intelligence, general self-efficacy, and perceived stress: Evidence from Thailand. *Journal of Spirituality in Mental Health*, 16(3), 171–92.

Cook-Sather, A., Bovill, C. and Felten, P. (2014). *Engaging Students as Partners in Learning and Teaching: A Guide for Faculty*. San Francisco, CA: Jossey-Bass.

Davis, A. J. (1984). Soloing: Body talk. *The American Journal of Nursing*, 84(7), 932–4.

Department for Education and Skills (2004). *Pedagogy and Practice: Teaching and Learning in Secondary Schools. Unit 5. Starters and Plenaries*. Available at: https://dera.ioe.ac.uk//5668/

Education Endowment Foundation (2019). *Voice 21: Oracy Curriculum, Culture and Assessment Toolkit*. Available at: https://educationendowmentfoundation.org.uk/projects-and-evaluation/projects/voice-21-pilot/

Fiedler, K., Walther, E., Freytag, P. and Plessner, H. (2002). Judgment biases in a simulated classroom: A cognitive–environmental approach. *Organizational Behavior and Human Decision Processes*, 88(1), 527–61.

Finn, M. (ed.) (2016). *The Gove Legacy: Education in Britain After the Coalition*. Basingstoke: Palgrave Macmillan.

Fisher, P. (2002). *Thinking through History*. Cambridge: Chris Kington Publishing.

Gladwell, M. (2008) *Outliers*. New York: Little Brown and Company.

Hagenauer, G., Hascher, T. and Volet, S. E. (2015). Teacher emotions in the classroom: Associations with students' engagement, classroom discipline and the interpersonal teacher-student relationship. *European Journal of Psychology of Education*, 30, 385–403.

Hanna, J. (2014). Connecting with sullen students: Using an emotionally honest classroom to reach out to disengaged students. *Clearing House*, 87(5), 224–8.

Hargreaves, A. (2005). The emotions of teaching and educational change. In: A. Hargreaves (ed.) *Extending Educational Change*. Dordrecht: Springer, pp. 278–95.

Jerrim, J., Taylor, H., Sims, S. and Allen, R. (2020). Has the mental health and wellbeing of teachers in England declined over time? New evidence from three datasets. *Oxford Review of Education*, 47(6), 805–25.

Johnson, D. W., Johnson, R. T. and Smith, K. (2007). The state of cooperative learning in postsecondary and professional settings. *Educational Psychology Review*, 19, 15–29.

Joyce, B., Weil, M. and Calhoun, E. (2003). *Models of Teaching* (7th edn). Boston: Allyn & Bacon.

Kabat-Zinn, J. (1994). *Wherever You Go, There You Are: Mindfulness Meditation in Everyday Life*. New York: Hyperion.

Kirschner, P. A. and Hendrick, C. (2020). *How Learning Happens: Seminal Works in Educational Psychology and What They Mean in Practice*. Abingdon: Routledge.

Knuppenburg, R. M. and Fredericks, C. M. (2021). Linguistic affect: Positive and negative emotion words are contagious, predict likability, and moderate positive and negative affect. *Inquiries Journal* [Online], 13. Available at: www.inquiriesjournal.com/a?id=1884

Kolb, D. (1984). *Experiential Learning: Experiences as the Source of Learning Development* (Vol. 1). Englewood Cliffs, NJ: Prentice-Hall.

Lister, K., Seale, J. and Douce, C. (2021). Mental health in distance learning: A taxonomy of barriers and enablers to student mental wellbeing. *Open Learning: The Journal of Open, Distance and e-Learning*. Available at: https://doi.org/10.1080/02680513.2021.1899907

Lucariello, J. and Naff, D. (2010). How do I get my students over their alternative conceptions (misconceptions) for learning? Applications of psychological science to teaching and learning modules. Removing barriers to aid in the development of the student. Available at: www.apa.org/education-career/k12/misconceptions

Maslow, A. H. (1943). A theory of human motivation. *Psychological Review*, 50(4), 430–37.

Mayer, J.D. and Salovey, P. (1997). *What Is Emotional Intelligence? Emotional Development and Emotional Intelligence: Implications for Educators*. Basic Books, New York, 3-31.

Shafer, L. (2018). What makes a good school culture? Available at: https://www.gse.harvard.edu/news/uk/18/07/what-makes-good-school-culture

Ofsted (2014). *Research and Analysis: Low-level Disruption in Classrooms: Below the Radar*. Available at: www.gov.uk/government/publications/below-the-radar-low-level-disruption-in-the-countrys-classrooms

Paivio, A. (1990). *Mental Representations: A Dual Coding Approach*. Oxford: Oxford University Press.

Pekrun, R. and Linnenbrink-Garcia, L. (eds) (2014). *International Handbook of Emotions in Education*. New York: Routledge.

Piaget, J. (1971). The theory of stages in cognitive development. In: D. R. Green, M. P. Ford and G. B. Flamer (eds) *Measurement and Piaget*. New York: McGraw-Hill.

Pigford, T. (2001). Improving teacher–student relationships: What's up with that? *Clearing House*, 74(6), 337–9.

Rainer, T. (1978/2004). *The New Diary: How to Use a Journal for Self-Guidance and Expanded Creativity*. New York: Jeremy P. Tarcher/Penguin.

Robson, D. (2020). *The Intelligence Trap: Revolutionise Your Thinking and Make Wiser Decisions*. London: Hodder & Stoughton.

Rowe, M. B. (1986). Wait time: Slowing down may be a way of speeding up! *Journal of Teacher Education*, 37(1), 43–50.

Schrum, L. and Hong, S. (2002, July). Dimensions and strategies for online success: Voices from experienced educators. *Journal of Asynchronous Learning Network*, 6(1), 57–67.

Schultz, K. (2012). The fullness of silence in the classroom. *Phi Delta Kappan*, 94(2), 80–80.

Thiran, R. (2018) It's not how you start that counts, it's how you finish. Available at: https://www.leaderonomics.com/articles/leadership/how-you-finish

Viafora, D. P., Mathiesen, S. G. and Unsworth, S. J. (2015). Teaching mindfulness to middle school students and homeless youth in school classrooms. *Journal of Child and Family Studies*, 24(5), 1179–91.

U. S. Army Board Study Guide. (2006). https://www.armystudyguide.com/wp-content/uploads/2017/11/Board_Study_Guide_5_0.pdf

Vygotsky, L. (1962). *Thought and Language*, ed. E. Hanfmann and G. Vakar. Cambridge, MA: MIT Press.

Vygotsky, L. S. (1978). *Mind in Society: The Development of Higher Psychological Processes*. Cambridge, MA: Harvard University Press.

Wenger, A. (2020). *My Life in Red and White*. London: Weidenfeld & Nicolson.

Wyeth, S. (2014). 10 ways great speakers capture people's attention. Available at: www.inc.com/sims-wyeth/how-to-capture-and-hold-audience-attention.html

INDEX